A Semester in
the Sandbox

A Semester in the Sandbox

A Marine Reservist's Iraq War Journal

Adam Davidson

McFarland & Company, Inc., Publishers
Jefferson, North Carolina

LIBRARY OF CONGRESS CATALOGUING-IN-PUBLICATION DATA

Names: Davidson, Adam, 1982– author.
Title: A semester in the sandbox : a Marine
reservist's Iraq War journal / Adam Davidson.
Other titles: Marine reservist's Iraq War journal
Description: Jefferson, North Carolina : McFarland &
Company, Inc., Publishers, 2016 | Includes index.
Identifiers: LCCN 2016031478 | ISBN 9781476665696
(pbk. : acid free paper) ∞
Subjects: LCSH: Davidson, Adam, 1982– —Diaries. | Iraq War,
2003–2011—Personal narratives, American. | Marines—United
States—Biography. | United States. Marine Corps Reserve.
Combat Engineer Battalion, 4th—Biography.
Classification: LCC DS79.766 .D36 2016 | DDC 956.7044/345 [B]—dc23
LC record available at https://lccn.loc.gov/2016031478

BRITISH LIBRARY CATALOGUING DATA ARE AVAILABLE

ISBN (print) 978-1-4766-6569-6
ISBN (ebook) 978-1-4766-2573-7

Front cover photograph: The author beside a pair of
artillery shell components of a large IED found along
Route Mobile. The device was composed of 28
artillery shells (author's photograph)

Printed in the United States of America

McFarland & Company, Inc., Publishers
Box 611, Jefferson, North Carolina 28640
www.mcfarlandpub.com

To the memories of Sergeant Jesse Strong,
Corporal Christopher Weaver, Corporal Jonathan Bowling,
Corporal Bradley Arms, and Lance Corporal Karl Linn

Contents

Acknowledgments

First and foremost, I want to thank the Marines of the 4th Combat Engineer Battalion, Charlie Company, specifically 2nd platoon. From the Captain and Staff Sergeants—who guided us and looked after our well being through the deployment—to each individual Marine. "We few, we happy few, we band of brothers; for he today that sheds his blood with me, shall be my brother"—Semper Fi.

I also want to thank Eric Danner, without whom I would not have completed this book. Both for his insights, contributions, and edits—as well as his guidance and support while I wrestled with the idea of publishing my private journal. Lastly, I would like to thank my family for supporting me and keeping me in your thoughts and prayers while I was deployed, as well as for your continued support—I couldn't have done it without you.

List of Terms

29 Palms Marine Corps base located in the Mojave Desert, CA
4th CEB 4th Combat Engineer Battalion
1/23 1st Battalion, 23rd Marine Regiment
.50 cal. Heavy machine gun, often mounted on a Humvee
AFB Air Force Base
ASP Ammunition Supply Point
AO Area of Operations
AT Advanced Training, two weeks of summer training for Reservists
BOLO List "Be on the lookout" list
CO Commanding Officer
EOD Explosive Ordnance Disposal
FLASH report A radio message of extreme urgency
FOB Forward Operating Base
Grunt Infantryman
Hajjis U.S. military slang for Iraqis
Hardback Humvee An enclosed Humvee with a turret
High-back Humvee An open-backed Humvee, similar to a pickup
    truck
HET Human Exploitation Team
IED Improvised Explosive Device
IM Instant Messenger
JBCC Joint Border Crossing Center
JSOC Joint Special Operations Command
KV FOB or **Camp Korean Village**—a U.S. base in Iraq
LAR Light Armored Reconnaissance
LAV Light Armored Vehicle, used by LAR
M16 Standard issue U.S. military rifle
M203 Grenade launcher, mounted on a rifle

M240G Medium machine gun, generally carried by a two-man team
MK19 Grenade launcher, usually mounted on a Humvee
Med-evac Medical evacuation
MOUT Military Operations in Urban Terrain
MSR Main Supply Route
Muj U.S. military slang for enemy fighters, short for Mujahedeen
MWR Morale, Welfare, and Recreation Center
NVG Night Vision Goggles
OP Observation Post
PT Physical Training
PTSD Post Traumatic Stress Disorder
PX Post Exchange, an on-base retail store
RPG Rocket Propelled Grenade
RPK Soviet-era machine gun
SAPI Plates Small Arms Protective Inserts, plates inserted into a
    flak jacket
Sapper Another name for a combat engineer
SASO Security and Stability Operations
SAW Squad Automatic Weapon, a light machine gun
Semtex Plastic explosives, similar to C4
SMAW Shoulder-launched Multipurpose Assault Weapon
SPOT report A radio message to provide a status report
SSgt Staff Sergeant
UXO Unexploded Ordnance
VBIED Vehicle Borne Improvised Explosive Device, a car bomb
VCP Vehicle Check Point

Preface

I came across my Iraq War journal while going through boxes in my parents' garage. At some point during my many moves after college, I had lost track of it, and after frantically searching for a number of years, had finally given up hope of finding it. It was the most exasperating feeling; I couldn't believe I had misplaced something so important to me. I had brought home few items from Iraq: an Iraqi Army helmet, a few dozen photos, a black insurgent hood found after an ambush. But my journal mattered more than all these others. I don't usually keep a journal, but during those months in Iraq it served as my closest confidant—a means to decompress, as well as a way to document everything I had been through. Upon returning to my squad's tent at base camp following a mission, I would lie on my bunk and scribble down everything that had happened in as much detail as possible. I didn't want to forget a single emotion or event.

As luck would have it, my journal wasn't lost. It spent five years stuffed in a shoebox underneath some pictures and letters. I don't know how it ended up there, but as I sat in the garage and flipped through the pages, I was transported back in time as I remembered people and events I had forgotten. Reading the journal is as close as I can get to reliving some of those experiences.

I was deployed to Iraq for seven months, from late 2004 to early 2005. Immediately after returning home, the time I spent there seemed to be the only thing that occupied my mind. Even after returning for my final year of college in the fall, nearly six months after my last combat mission, I found myself struggling to focus in class as my thoughts would drift back to the war. I would reminisce and even feel nostalgic about the good times, while struggling to keep myself from letting the darker memories weigh too heavily. I found this particularly difficult in the first few months following my deployment. Reservists, unlike their active duty brethren, completely detach from the military when they jump back into civilian life after a deployment. While the military has gone through great effort to provide a suitable period of decompression following a deployment, there is no getting around the fact that the transition is jarring. Suddenly, I found myself surrounded by people who had no concept of what I had been doing just a short time ago. Initially it was an incredibly isolating and lonely feeling, particularly on a college campus that could not have felt further from Iraq. But eventually, the memories began to fade from my daily thoughts. Not that I could ever completely forget, but like all memories, they began to be slowly overshadowed by day-to-day concerns, until I would rarely catch myself thinking about Iraq at all. Now, more than ten years later, it seems a distant memory. So as I flipped through my rediscovered journal, it was almost as if someone else was talking to me. Most of the memories were still there but, surprisingly, many had faded, blurred, or morphed.

Reading the journal, I began to realize there was something unique in these pages. I make no claims of being a stellar writer, particularly in a journal not planned for public consumption. But I made a concerted effort to meticulously document the details of my deployment. I wrote down everything, from what I was doing to what I was feeling. While deployed, I imagined that I was writing to my future grandchildren, or great-grandchildren—wanting them to understand who I was and what I had lived through. It relates my personal experiences, so for this reason my journal is special to me. But as I reread it, it dawned on me that it could be of interest to others for alternate reasons. It's a complete and un-glamorized account of a deployment to Iraq from the perspective of a combat-arms Marine Reservist, from the first notification of mobilization to the final trip home. For people who didn't experience the wars in Iraq or Afghanistan, there is a natural curiosity about these two complex and unique conflicts. In many ways this journal typifies the experience that thousands of service men and women have lived through. Iraq, as of now, remains mired in conflict. To this day, the United States is embroiled in that troubled country, with servicemen and women engaged against militant groups that grew mainly out of the Iraq War. Of course there are already dozens of accounts of the

2

Iraq War written by politicians, generals, snipers, and Special Forces operatives—but there haven't been many written by the average enlisted combat Marine or soldier. Even more rare, is an account written from the perspective of the Reserve Forces of the U.S. military.

I can't put my finger on exactly why I made this effort to document my deployment. At the time I assumed my journal would be nothing more than a piece of personal history to pass on to my children. Before I even reported for duty, I knew that this experience would be life altering, and that I should make every effort to record it. This journal captures my experience in a way that I could never hope to replicate from memory. What it lacks in polished prose is made up for in candid details of visceral experiences. I can't relive the stress, boredom, excitement, fear, and sadness that prompted me to write these words. Only in an account never meant to be viewed by others could I have been so frank.

* * *

I've always been fascinated by military history, especially first-person accounts. Unlike dry history books that lists events and dates, these accounts are like the people that write them—unique. They offer a personal perspective and context which even the most meticulously analyzed histories cannot. Written as the events they describe are actually unfolding, first-person accounts allow the reader to live the story alongside the writer. A natural byproduct is that they are often filled with the rumors and hearsay of the time. But I feel this only adds to their charm. Unlike memoirs, as you read a journal the future is uncertain to both the reader and the writer—the ending is unknown. This journal offers a glimpse into my time as a Marine Reservist who, like countless others, was called from my college campus to serve on the battlefields of Iraq. A reader looking for an action-packed military account may be slightly disappointed. I was not in Baghdad or Fallujah, but rather a dusty little corner of Iraq's western Al Anbar province. But I can tell you what happened in that place from August 2004 to March 2005 in a way that no journalist, politician, or detailed history of the war could. It's a story of combat, homesickness, boredom, and loss that has become all too common to the warriors of this modern conflict.

I decided to incorporate all of my journal entries, leaving nothing out with the exception of altering a few names and locations to protect individual privacy, as well as the identities of our Iraqi translators and informants. In addition, I made an effort to selectively correct grammar, spell out some acronyms, and occasionally add clarifying sentences in order to improve readability and avoid confusion. Sometimes, the journal refers to articles and news clippings sent from home. Often these articles describe events that I either personally witnessed or heard of secondhand. The juxtaposition between my perspective and the articles provides an interesting snapshot into the reality of events versus how they are described in the media or, for that matter, by the rumor mill of enlisted Marines. As is often the case, the truth generally lies somewhere in between. My objective in publishing this journal is not to insult anyone's character or stir any kind of controversy. After all, these are my observations and opinions at a certain point in time, without the benefit of foresight. I was in my early twenties and many thoughts and statements no longer reflect my current thinking.

The journal begins on the first day of our unit being called to active duty. I enlisted in the Marine Corps in August 2000, two months after my high school graduation. I could write volumes about what prompted me to enlist, but will sum it up by simply saying I was looking for a challenge and adventure. In the pre–9/11 world an enlistment in the Marine Reserves carried much less risk than in subsequent years. Having deferred my college admission for a year, I shipped out for the legendary U.S. Marine Corps Recruit Depot at Parris Island, South Carolina in January 2001. After just over three months of boot camp, I reported to Camp Lejeune in North Carolina for three months of additional training. This training included seventeen days of Marine Combat Training, an abridged version of infantry school, and my occupational specialty training as a combat engineer. Shortly before starting college in the fall of 2001, I completed my training in North Carolina and officially joined my Reserve unit, "C" or "Charlie" Company of the 4th Combat Engineer Battalion, located in Lynchburg, Virginia. The selection of my Reserve unit was more of an afterthought in the enlistment process. It seemed to be the nearest Marine Reserve unit to my college, in addition to being only a few hours from my hometown. I signed up for the Marine Reserves with a commitment to serve one weekend a month and two weeks each summer for a period of six years with, of course, the caveat that I could be called to active service at any time and for any duration. My original intention was to go into the active duty Marine Corps as an officer after finishing college and I thought the experience of boot camp, along with several years as an enlisted Marine in the Reserves, would put me well ahead of my peers in the officer candidate selection process.

I was still one of the new guys in the unit, having attended only one of the weekend training sessions, prior to the attacks of September 11, 2001. The first I heard of the events of that day was as I was returning to my dorm room from a morning class. I became increasingly alarmed as everyone I passed asked if I had seen the news and I spent the day, like most Americans, transfixed by the footage on TV. A little later in the day, I received a call from my squad leader. He was merely calling to check in, but it served as a jarring reminder that I might no longer be just an observer of world events. I anxiously waited for the call to mobilize following the invasion of Afghanistan, but the rapid fall of the Taliban dashed our hopes of being part of an invasion force. As the months passed, the sense of urgency about a deployment seemed to ease and I fell into the routine of attending the monthly drill weekends. In the summer of 2002, Charlie Company spent two weeks involved in a combined-arms training exercise at 29 Palms in the Mojave Desert of California. Meanwhile, the possibility of a deployment to Afghanistan as part of the occupation began to appear less and less likely.

As 2002 rolled into 2003, tensions again began to increase as all talk turned to Iraq. War began to seem inevitable, so we again readied ourselves for a possible deployment; but again the call did not come. Though no one wanted to be uprooted from their jobs, schools or families, I believe we all felt a slight sense of disappointment. Not that we were particularly concerned about a perceived need to play our part in eradicating WMDs—rather, there was a slight sense of embarrassment of being in a combat-arms Marine unit and having never been called to active service following the attacks of September 11. I certainly wasn't eager to leave home or school for a deployment to Iraq or Afghanistan but when people found out that I was a Marine, they inevitably asked if I had been overseas, to which I could only sheepishly answer "not yet."

Instead of being part of the invasion of Iraq, I skipped class to watch TV as Coalition artillery announced the beginning of a new war. Initially we thought that Iraq would play out much the same as Afghanistan, but after several months it became apparent that things were unfolding very differently. U.S. troops were meeting large-scale opposition and, as invasion settled into occupation, the pace of the conflict didn't seem to slacken. A combination of ex-Ba'athists, Iraqi nationalists, Islamists, and foreign fighters began to reconsolidate after being battered during the invasion, and the levels of violence began to steadily increase. Nevertheless, the call for our unit to mobilize never came. In the summer of 2003, we spent our two-week training period in Romania conducting joint exercises with foreign militaries from southeastern Europe. As with Afghanistan, the months began to roll by and, despite the distinctly higher levels of violence, we began to doubt that the call would come.

As the summer of 2004 approached, I was less focused on Iraq and more focused on preparing to study abroad in Germany. Prior to leaving for Germany, while fishing at home, a friend asked if I was concerned about the potential of being deployed. It seems naive in retrospect, but at the time it wasn't even on my mind. Of course it seemed possible, but with so many troops having been withdrawn after the invasion, I doubted that there would be a need to mobilize a large number of Reserve units. I was more than a little shocked when, after only two short weeks in Germany, the call finally came. I was traveling prior to the start of classes when my parents contacted me through German relatives, asking that I give them a call. I knew something must be wrong but, even then, assumed that perhaps a grandparent was ill. It seems laughable now, but I was truly blindsided. It was with a mixture of both concern and excitement that I flew back to the U.S. to report to my unit.

I was eager to know exactly when and where our unit would be going. What kind of missions would we be doing? How long would we be there? It sounds ludicrous now but at the time my biggest concern was that we would be sent to some rear base where I would be stuck doing months of guard duty, which, to my thinking at the time, would be almost as embarrassing as not going at all. As I had learned early in my time in the Marines, information is always in short supply. We were only told that we would be shipping out in order to support Operation Iraqi Freedom. The rumor mill circulated and the consensus was that we would be departing in a couple months, probably sometime in August or September. Exactly where in Iraq was anyone's guess. However, we all knew that most Marine units were serving in Iraq's Al Anbar province, a largely Sunni Muslim region in the western part of the country and the epicenter of the Sunni insurgency.

The media filed daily reports of pitched battles between Marines and insurgents in the province. Fallujah had become instantly recognizable to the average American following the highly publicized massacre of a convoy of Blackwater contractors in the spring of 2004, and the subsequent U.S. assaults on the city. Ramadi, the provincial capital, was also known as a hotbed of insurgent activity. I recall looking at a map of the province prior to our deployment and registering some concern as I recognized a number of place names—a bad sign considering I had only known of Baghdad prior to the war. It began to dawn on me that we would most likely see action and that there was a high probability we would not all be coming home. Iraq was a very dangerous place in 2004, and we would be heading right into the middle of it.

Charlie Company conducted two weeks of hastily prepared summer training, which fell under our standard Reserve commitment, before officially reporting for active duty on July 5, 2004. Between these two weeks spent in Lynchburg and nearby Fort A.P. Hill, we had a few precious days off to spend with friends and family. They passed in a blur. I tried to spend as much time with my family as possible. I also drove to college to clear out my room and have one last party with friends who would be graduating while I was away. While driving home, I parked along the York River to call my good friend Scott Miles who, having recently finished his six year enlistment in the Reserves, was struggling with the question of whether he should reenlist in order to deploy with us. Not surprisingly, given his character, Miles did reenlist. At this early stage, while I assumed our unit would suffer some casualties, it never seemed to register that I would *personally* be in any danger. I was certainly naïve, but it just didn't feel that real yet. Of course I was sad to leave my friends and family but not because I thought there was a possibility that I would never see them again. I was more concerned and disappointed to miss graduating from college with my friends; the thought that I may not come back didn't seriously cross my mind.

I spent an uncomfortable 4th of July with my parents and sisters in Lynchburg. In order to spend time together, we had arrived a couple days prior to when I would be reporting to my unit. While there we tried to have as much fun as we could, but there was a dark cloud hanging over everything we did. As soon as I would start to enjoy myself, something in the back of my mind would remind me that I would be leaving soon, and I would experience a sinking feeling in the pit of my stomach. Despite this, or perhaps because of it, I was ready to get going. I was a little nervous and sad to be leaving my family but, from my perspective, on the 5th of July I would be joining my friends to start training for the deployment— this was just the beginning of a new adventure, not necessarily an ending. I was as excited as I was nervous. My family, on the other hand, would be driving home from Lynchburg to a slightly emptier house; with months of anxiety and stress ahead of them. Even when I was safely asleep in my bunk in Iraq, they would have no idea if at that very moment, their only son was fighting for his life. As difficult as it was for me to say goodbye, I knew that this would be one of the hardest things they would ever have to endure. More than anything, I felt an overriding sense of guilt for what I was putting them through. When it came time to say our final goodbyes, I was glad to finally get it over with and get going.

Shortly after reporting for duty, Charlie Company was flown to California for training and exercises to be held at Camp Pendleton, 29 Palms, and March Air Force Base. I began to write in my journal consistently around this time, until my final entry for the training period was made April 1, 2005. Prior to mobilization, I made a promise to myself to document everything I could—every emotion, every conversation, and every event. I wasn't sure where we would go or what would happen to us over the next year, only that it would be important for me to write it all down. It's funny how what seems like such a monumental event in one's life is, in all reality, just a very tiny part of what will one day be a footnote in the history books. I had no illusions that we were embarking on anything great or even worthwhile, but at that point I didn't care. I had made a commitment to serve when called and, more importantly, I was committed to the friends alongside whom I would be serving.

Charlie Company and the Early Period of the Iraq War

Even before the invasion of Iraq there was the expectation on the part of many American policymakers, as well as the public, that the war would be wrapped up quickly. This stemmed in large part from what some in the military perceived as pressure from the Bush administration to produce artificially low troop estimates during the run-up to the war. Army Chief of Staff General Eric Shinseki argued that to successfully secure Iraq following the invasion, the United States would require a force comparable to that of Desert Storm—at least several hundred thousand troops. Donald Rumsfeld publicly questioned this position and implied that Shinseki's estimate was flawed and pessimistic. His deputy, Paul Wolfowitz, in an appearance before the House Budget Committee claimed that Shinseki's post-invasion troop numbers were wildly off the mark, and went so far as to question the logic underlying the notion that providing post-invasion security would require more troops than the invasion itself.

To have the civilian leadership of the Department of Defense publicly and pointedly question the judgment of the Chief of Staff of the Army represented something of a departure from the history of military planning in the United States. Even so, the Bush administration pressed on with its small-footprint strategy and ultimately sent an invasion force of 145,000 troops, along with token contingents from several other countries. Not surprisingly, the Iraqi Army proved no match for the invasion force and, by and large, put up little in the way of organized resistance—it took only three weeks for Baghdad to fall. To govern the newly-freed Iraq, Bush appointed L. Paul Bremer as Presidential Envoy and head of the Coalition Provisional Authority, the interim national governing body.

Though the Coalition was successful in removing Saddam Hussein and his security apparatus, it lacked the troop strength—or the orders—to secure government infrastructure beyond key facilities such as oil refineries, military bases, and a handful of government ministries. In short order this resulted in looting on a grand scale, along with a rapid and complete deterioration of civil order. This problem was exacerbated by Bremer's decision to disband and stop paying the Iraqi army—despite the fact that some in the Pentagon had planned to use a pacified Iraqi army to help provide security. Instead, these hundreds of thousands of men returned home with their weapons, but without jobs or realistic prospects for the future. This contributed to a situation that was quickly escalating into a full insurrection. In the hope of bringing about a political solution to the nascent insurgency, along with some measure of reconciliation, the Bush administration sought to hold elections in order to draft a new constitution. These elections were to be held in January 2005 and were considered, by both the U.S. and the insurgency, as a bellwether of the potential for Iraq to heal its rifts and move forward as a cohesive, unified nation. With the country in political and social upheaval, it was largely left to the U.S. military to maintain law and order. It was a confused and chaotic Iraq into which we would be deploying.

* * *

Company C, or Charlie Company, of the 4th Combat Engineer Battalion (CEB) is comprised of approximately one hundred fifty Marines from the Lynchburg, Virginia area. There has been a Marine Reserve unit based in Lynchburg, a small city in south-central Virginia, since the Korean War. Initially a rifle company, the unit eventually picked up the mantle of the 4th CEB, a battalion that has its origins in World War II. The 4th CEB had been deactivated following the conclusion of that war, only to be reinstated during the Korean War. Since the Korean War, the 4th CEB has been a permanent part of the U.S. Marine Corp Reserve Forces with companies currently based in Virginia, West Virginia, Tennessee, and Maryland. The conventional duties of combat engineers can be summarized simply as: performing

missions that impede the movement of the enemy, while simultaneously enhancing the mobility of our own troops. This is a broad man-
date and in a traditional conflict can include everything from assembling
prefabricated bridges, to planting and clearing minefields, constructing
and destroying fortifications, and using demolitions to breach enemy
buildings and strong points. Essentially, anything that can allow our
troops to move as quickly as possible, while simultaneously slowing
and channeling the enemy's movement. When the Cold War posed the
very real prospect of facing down massive Soviet armored divisions,
the role of combat engineers was considered extremely important. Even
as recently as the Gulf War, combat engineers were heavily used to
blast the way through enemy minefields and obstacles.

When mobilized, combat engineers are generally integrated into
the infantry or other combat arms units, which they've been designated
to support. This results in the engineer unit being split into pieces and
essentially becoming integrated as part of the infantry's chain of command, allowing the infantry commanders the ability to quickly utilize
their engineer assets in order to exploit an opportunity. Weekends of
Reserve training with Charlie Company ranged across a number of
combat engineer functions, in addition to the standard training required
of all Marines such as rifle qualification, physical fitness testing, and
swim qualification. However, the primary focus of Charlie Company
was always on the core duties of combat engineers. We learned how
to set explosive charges on trees in order to make obstacles across
roads, trained in the various means of clearing a path through minefields, and built barbed wire impediments in order to practice blasting
our way through them. All of these skills are extremely important in
conventional, mobile warfare. The ability to funnel enemy troop for-
mations into our killing fields by use of fortifications, minefields, and
obstacles can have devastating effects. When the call "engineers up"
crackles over the radio, combat engineers are expected to break through
whatever obstacles the command is facing.

After the initial outbreak of hostilities in Iraq, Marine combat
engineers performed their traditional functions expertly. However, by
2004 the Iraq War had devolved from a fairly conventional war of
mobility to a police action primarily set in an urban environment, ren-
dering the majority of our training useless. There were no bridges to

destroy and, if the enemy could be found at all, there were few obstacles to breach. Despite this, combat engineers still possessed some vital skills of tactical value in this modern, asymmetrical battlefield. Specifically, we focused on honing and expanding our knowledge of urban breaching. While still being expected to handle the occasional land-mine, Military Operations in Urban Terrain (MOUT) became the primary focus of training. We learned the various explosive charges used to gain entry into buildings, along with the calculations to determine the minimum standoff distance from detonations. We spent long hours training on how to make the charges and how to methodically clear a building after having breached it. We also learned the various methods of patrolling in cities, as well as how to conduct the raids and urban assaults in which we would utilize these urban breaching skills. A consequence of our usefulness being restricted to these specific areas meant that combat engineers could expect to be employed in some of the most combat-heavy missions. Nearly every raid or assault on a known enemy target was led or supported by combat engineers with the ability to breach obstacles and appear where the enemy least expected.

Charlie Company was separated into three platoons, each containing roughly thirty to forty Marines. Upon mobilization, each platoon was to be attached to support a different infantry battalion and, at the platoon level, each squad of ten to twelve Marines was to be assigned to support an infantry company. I was a member of 2nd Platoon, led by our platoon commander Captain Kuniholm—a relatively recent addition to the unit. In reality, as with most Marine combat arms units, the day-to-day operations of our platoon were run by the two senior non-commissioned officers (NCOs): Staff Sergeants Dreany and Saxo. Jokingly referred to as the Dad and Mom of the platoon, Dreany had a stern, businesslike approach while Saxo, equally as diligent, had a softer touch. Whereas Dreany might scold a mistake, Saxo would ask what went wrong. It was a perfect combination of personalities, with both NCOs being exceptionally professional Marines who took their responsibility to heart. If anyone may be under the illusion that Reservists only dedicate one weekend a month to training, then they should think again. Dreany and Saxo were a testament to the fact that the time commitment to a Reserve unit, particularly during a time of war, can rival that of a full time job.

Second Platoon was further broken into three squads, with a fourth added later. I was a member of the 2nd Squad, led by Sergeant Wallace. Within 2nd Squad we were separated into two fire-teams, the first led directly by Sergeant Wallace and the second, to which I belonged, led by Corporal GG. At the time of our deployment, I had been with the platoon for nearly three years and, over that time, had developed some close friendships. In my experience, Charlie Company was a unique group of Marines. Located central to a number of universities, over half of the platoon was composed of either current college students or recent graduates. Marines from the company were enrolled at the Virginia Military Institute, Virginia Tech, Liberty University, Virginia Commonwealth University, Appalachian State, the

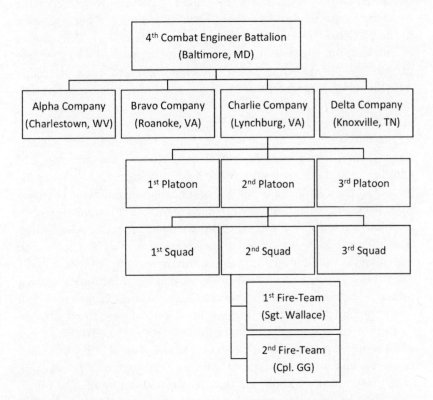

The organizational structure of the 4th Combat Engineer Battalion and Charlie Company.

University of Virginia, and James Madison University. Those in the professional world ranged from truck drivers and fast food workers to lawyers and defense contractors. However, with so many coming from similar backgrounds, it wasn't long before we formed a strong bond. Although it wasn't uncommon to gripe about the hurry-up-and-wait nature of drill weekends, most of us looked forward to the chance to spend time with guys who had become good friends.

By the time of our deployment, the insurgency had consolidated and was becoming more organized and lethal in its attacks on Coalition troops. The insurgents, alternately referred to as Hajjis or Muj by Marines, had begun operating with a renewed vigor and higher level of sophistication. The idea of "Mission Accomplished" and the prospects of a peaceful transition had all but faded. Casualties were increasing significantly due in particular to the lethality of a relatively new weapon to the battlefield, the improvised explosive device (IED). The dangers of this weapon, whether as a roadside bomb or packed into a vehicle driven by a suicide bomber, were quickly impressed upon us. While not officially falling under the duties of a combat engineer, our special-ized training in explosives meant that early in the war, engineers were often called upon to deal with unexploded IEDs.

In addition to IEDs, Iraq was still littered with thousands of land-mines from the Iraq-Iran War and Desert Storm. These minefields, in addition to vast quantities that were held in storage, had been appro-priated by the insurgents as law and order collapsed following the inva-sion. Sweeping for landmines with metal detectors falls squarely within a combat engineer's purview and, if the person laying the mine knows what they are doing, can be equally as dangerous as an IED. Similar to sweeping for landmines, discovering enemy weapons caches, usually materials such as artillery shells used for making IEDs, also became a primary responsibility of engineers. These weapons caches were full of equipment pilfered from Iraqi Army depots during the confusion that followed the invasion. In addition to artillery shells, the caches often included mortar shells, crates of ammo, light and heavy weapons, grenades, and any other type of military hardware readily available in the free-for-all of 2003. Eliminating these caches, typically found hidden in buildings or buried, was considered critical to starving the insurgency of the weaponry needed to fight Coalition troops. These duties, coupled with combat engineers' prominent role in urban combat, had led to significant casualties in engineer units prior to Charlie Company's deployment. Casualty rates averaged around 15 percent—one of the highest of all military occupational specialties.

After reporting for duty on July 5, a few days were spent in Lynchburg before Charlie Company was shipped to Camp Pendleton in California for advanced combat engineer training at the Sapper School. All of the instructors at the Sapper School were veteran combat engineers, recently returned from Iraq. For anyone who wasn't already impressed by the seriousness of our situation, the commander of the 1st Combat Engineer Battalion, based at Camp Pendleton, provided a wakeup call when he greeted us with the warning that his battalion had suffered significant casualties in Iraq and that we could expect the same. I recall looking around our platoon, thinking about the possibility that more than one-in-ten would not be returning home in one piece. While many outwardly shrugged it off as a scare tactic to ensure that we remained diligent in our training, we all inwardly understood the gravity of the situation. Perhaps more poignantly, one of our instructors at the Sapper School was a Marine recently returned from medical leave after having lost his eye to a landmine in Iraq. It was quickly made clear that we didn't have time for a full dress rehearsal. After five or six weeks of training, we would be shipping out to an active war zone where we were all but guaranteed to see combat. It was a sobering prospect.

The first part of my journal primarily details our training process in California prior to our deployment. The entries during this period reflect the nervous stress and energy under which we were operating. Our instructors pushed us hard in order to prepare us as much as possible in an extremely short amount of time. We fell into a routine of waking early for physical training, followed by classes or field instruction until evening. This process was repeated day after day with no break but for once, there was no griping or complaining. We all knew that we would only have a few short weeks for practice before we would be required to do the real thing in situations where our lives, or those of our friends, would depend upon our training. If there was one thing that kept me focused during the endless hours of classroom time, it was the knowledge that if I didn't pay attention it could cost someone's life.

July 2004–August 2004: Mobilizing

Lynchburg, VA
July 6, 2004

The goodbyes the other day were hard, much worse than I expected. Really, the whole time leading up to the fifth was tough. On the plus side, I was able to spend time with nearly everyone, but in a way, I'm almost glad it's over. The tension surrounding everything was mentally exhausting. The finality of every interaction—the last time going fishing with Dad, the last time grilling out with the family, the last beer with friends—made it all so gloomy. Making such an effort to enjoy the time together made everything just feel awkward and forced. I had thought it over before we got to the Drill Center and planned on just tearing off the Band-Aid: say my goodbyes quickly and get into formation. There was no point in belaboring the process, it would have just made it that much more difficult. For the most part, that's how it worked out, although it was still far from pleasant. I've never seen Dad get upset about anything, ever. I hadn't seen much reaction from him about my deployment until we were finally driving to the Drill Center. Mom and the girls went in the other car, while he and I went in the van. I could tell he was upset, and I wasn't sure what I should say or do. Thinking about that still makes my heart ache. I try to put things in perspective, but just because thousands of families are going through the same thing, or the fact that sending sons off to war has existed since the birth of nations, isn't much of a personal comfort. I can only imagine how difficult it was for the guys in the unit who have kids. Saying goodbye to your children, knowing that you're going to miss a year of their lives, must be one of the toughest things to ask of a parent.

At any rate, it sounds like things will be moving pretty quickly from here on out. We should be heading to California soon to start our pre-deployment training at Camp Pendleton. I'm sure it'll all be useful, but I'm anxious to just get the show on the road. My hope is that the training process will be wrapped up in a few weeks instead of dragging on for two or three months. As of now, we've been given no indication of when we'll actually be deploying in-country.

San Mateo, Camp Pendleton, CA
July 14, 2004

It feels like it's been a long time since I said good-bye, though it hasn't even been two weeks. If this is any indication, it's going to be a seriously long year. I'm not off to a great start of keeping this journal up-to-date, but we've been kept pretty busy, so it's been hard to find the time. My concerns about having a long training period before deploying were unfounded, as we found out that we'll be deploying sometime next month. This knowledge has helped with the sense of urgency in everything we do. While I wanted to deploy quickly, I think we all feel like we're playing catch-up in terms of getting prepared. We should have known that this was coming but, for some reason, our training was never really tailored specifically for Iraq until now. In fact, it was never really tailored for insurgencies in general. Hindsight is 20/20, but it seems like that should have been the first priority when a war kicked off that presented the clear potential for our unit to be mobilized. Instead, we kept training on the same stuff we'd always done. One of the last drill weekends before I left for Germany, we spent the entire time placing anti-tank landmines—what the hell were they thinking?

Thus far, the schedule has been extremely busy, but not too terrible. We've fallen into a routine of waking up, getting into formation outside of the barracks for PT (which is usually a run), showering, rushing through the chow hall, and then heading straight to the classroom. Classes usually last until lunch, which is followed by either more classes or practical application until dinner. By the end of the day we're all pretty tired, although sometimes a few of us still hit the gym in the evenings. It's a full day, but there's really not much else to do at San Mateo other than read or hang around the barracks, so it's best to be kept busy. Some guys drink at night, but the SSgts have started to crack down on it. Some guys clearly can't handle having a couple beers at the end of the day. One of the Preese brothers punched his hand through a window while drunk the other night. The SSgts protected him from getting into any serious trouble, but I think that move has likely ruined it for the rest of the guys. One consistent topic of evening conversation centers around gear and what non-issued stuff everyone plans on ordering. We've all bought three-point slings for our rifles, and I've got some kneepads coming my way, but am holding off on anything else. One of the instructors mentioned that the ground in Iraq is usually filthy and covered in broken glass and garbage. As we patrol, we'll be kneeling down all the time to take cover, so it made sense to order a pair. It seems so logical, but no one had mentioned it to us before. I guess all of us, officers and NCOs included, are learning as we go.

While the pace of training isn't too terrible, I'm not sure if it can last all the way until we deploy—at least not without a day or two off. People are going to get burnt out after a few weeks. While the sense of urgency is obviously present and no one is slacking, it's hard to maintain this level of intensity week after week. Besides, after a certain point, you can't retain information unless you have a mental rest. The only downside with an off day is that, although Camp Pendleton is a huge base, we're stuck on one small part of it. It's pretty isolated, with just a chow hall, a bunch of barracks, a small shop, and the classroom buildings. So a day off in this place wouldn't do us much good. That said, it's a really pretty area, and I wouldn't mind having a day to hike around. I haven't seen much of California outside of military bases but, from everything I've seen, it looks nice. At least the weather is great. You can just barely catch a glimpse of the ocean in the distance. Unfortunately, it's too far away to get to without a car, even if we did have a day off. Still, it makes for pretty scenery and beats the humidity of Virginia. There are some big houses up on the hills overlooking the ocean. It's strange to think that there are a bunch of rich lawyers and what not living in those homes. I'm sure they probably have strong opinions about the war one way or the other, but when you're that rich, it's unlikely to have any actual connection to it. While that doesn't mean they can't or shouldn't have an opinion, unless they have an ideological child that has signed up, the war probably won't impact their lives in any significant way.

The training has been good, all things considered. The instructors put in some serious hours. Considering that they probably have families, I'd say they are definitely going above and beyond in order to get us ready. We've had classes that go until 2000 hours, only to get up the next morning and have classes again first thing. We've been doing everything from communications classes to practicing with the new mine detectors, the 14s. The 14s are replacing the Vietnam-era 12s but seem a lot more complicated to operate and are somewhat finicky. Sometimes you shouldn't mess with what works—that seems to be the consensus so far. I can already see these as being a potential pain in the ass once we're deployed. We've also done a whole lot of "casualty evacuation" drills, which is military jargon for carrying each other up and down a football-size field. Apparently it came about as a result of Captain Kuniholm telling the instructors that he wanted them to "not waste any of our training time." I didn't actually hear him say it, but that's the rumor. If that is the case, then I don't think he'll mention it again. They smoked the shit out of us for a solid couple of hours the other day. I thought we would be done by dinner, but they had us come back for more. We were doing different crawls around the field, some while carrying gear and others while carrying a person. Really miserable, although I don't think anyone puked. Johnson kept us laughing part of the time by shouting and sounding off while running up and down the field.

The plus side of all of this training is that I've been doing better in morning PT. I had been pretty consistent with lifting regularly at school, but haven't spent enough time running. It's not too bad when you're with a group, but I just can't get motivated to run by myself. For better or worse, the SSgts are whipping us into shape. This morning, they ran us about six-and-a-half miles up the mountain and back. It was tough but also somewhat rewarding. The pace up the mountain slowed to a semi-jog or speed walk and, at times, we had to use our hands to scramble up sections. But it was beautiful at the top, the sun hadn't burned away the morning mist yet. We took a short break there, jogging in a circle while waiting for the slower guys to catch up. The only thing I could see were the other hilltops sticking out above the clouds. The rising sun lit everything above the clouds, and through breaks in the cover, I could see everything below was still dark and grey.

SSgt Saxo complimented my running this afternoon, which was nice to hear. He is, without a doubt, the best runner in the platoon, and maybe in the entire company. I need some reassurance that I'm doing well, especially since I lost my position as fire-team leader. There was the possibility that GG wasn't going to deploy, but now that he's joined back up with us, they had to give him the team since he outranks me. Besides, he had been the squad leader until being replaced by Wallace after the platoon was reorganized. Still, I can't help but feel like I'm moving backwards. Meyers said that the Staff Sergeants would rather have given me the squad if they could. If true, then it's nice to hear. But for better or worse, in the military, the deciding factor will always default to rank. At times, it doesn't always seem to be the best way. At least in the lower enlisted ranks you tend to get promoted based on how long you've been in, so as long as you don't screw up, you pick up rank on a fairly standardized schedule. Merit isn't really taken into account until the higher ranks, unless you're either a real screw up or shit-hot. I've read that the British Army is much more discerning about promotions; guys can stay a corporal or sergeant for the length of their career. Still, I count myself lucky that both my squad leader and fire-team leader are good guys. I can't imagine going to war with someone leading you that you don't like or trust.

Even though it has already felt like a long time, I'm not yet feeling homesick. Our schedule is too busy and I'm too excited about what's going to happen next, so there's no time to think about it. The only pang of homesickness I've had has been while standing in line in the chow hall the other day. A commercial came on the TV with a woman singing "You Are My Sunshine" in the background. I suddenly almost felt like crying and had to think of something else until the commercial was over—especially the line "please don't take my sunshine away." When I thought about it, I realized that I didn't have that reaction necessarily because I'm upset about leaving my family. It was more the knowledge of how difficult this will be for them. I feel guilty for putting them through this. What makes it worse is that I'm kind of looking forward to it. For better or worse, this will probably be one of the most interesting adventures of my life; it'd be crazy not to be somewhat excited.

San Mateo, Camp Pendleton, CA
July 15, 2004

Nothing much new today. We had more classes on patrolling with that strange, hyperactive instructor, Sergeant Moose. His lectures always seem to turn into weird rants. Parrott got chewed out for throwing rocks while we practiced patrolling around the barracks. They said he wasn't taking it seriously but, in all fairness, the training was pretty lame. It's hard to feel like you're really patrolling in a hostile environment when there's no one even playing the role of a potential enemy, or any mock hostile action that you're trying to observe. They could have at least buried some mock IEDs. I don't think Sergeant Moose knew how to react to Parrott's response to being yelled at. When he started chewing him out, Parrott snapped to attention and began sounding off like he was in boot camp, screaming "yes sir," "no sir," and "aye, sir." It was funny to those of us who know him, but you could tell that Sergeant Moose was proud of himself—he thought he'd scared Parrott shitless.

The commanding officer of the 1st CEB gave us a little "pep talk," in which he said that they've been suffering an average of fifteen percent casualties in Iraq. Fifteen percent aren't very good odds when you're talking about winning a bet, but when you're talking about keeping your life or limbs intact, it takes on a whole different meaning. I guess up until now I had assumed that we would all be coming home. Or that in the worst-case scenario, maybe one guy in the entire company could be hurt or killed. To be honest, I guess I haven't really thought about it that much. As I look around the platoon, statistically there will be four to five killed or wounded. It still doesn't seem real. I can't imagine what it will be like if and when it happens, especially if it's one of the guys that has been in 2nd Platoon since I joined. We've all gotten pretty close over the years. It hasn't taken long to get to know most of the guys that have recently joined as well. I can't even remember the rest of his speech. I just kept thinking about how this isn't going to be as easy as I thought.

Late today, SSgt Saxo asked if I would be willing to go with the advanced party from our platoon to Iraq, probably around August fifteenth. I said I would. We expect to finish our training out at 29 Palms and, we've been told, we'll likely get a couple days off once we get there. Going with the advanced party would mean that I wouldn't get those days off, but I think I'm OK with that. The days off would be nice, and I know more training is probably a good thing, but I'm just anxious to get over there and get started. He said I could expect to be in-country a week or two before the rest of the platoon arrives. The idea being that we would get the lay of the land and start going out on missions with the unit that we'll be replacing. Then, after the rest of the platoon arrives, we'll be a little experienced and can guide them as we start to run missions. I may be reading too much into the SSgt's request, but being picked for advanced party seems to be a pat on the back. I don't think they would ask someone that they thought to be incapable. I just hope that I have the chance to shine at some point in this deployment. Unless we take casualties, as a junior corporal, I likely won't be stepping into a leadership role. Getting picked for advance party would seem to be a move in the right direction.

San Mateo, Camp Pendleton, CA
July 17, 2004

Training has continued at a steady pace. Some has been good—particularly weapons training and landmine identification. While we've had a decent amount of training in *placing* landmines through our Reserve weekends, I don't think I've ever had any training on *identifying* enemy landmines, or at least not since engineer school. Other training hasn't been so good—like land navigation. Not that it's not useful stuff, but I find it hard to believe that we'll be wandering around Iraq with a map and compass. It's more likely that we'll be in a city and will have a GPS. I know you can't rely 100% on technology, but it still seems like a waste of our very limited time. We did a land navigation course during the day, followed by a night course. The daytime one went OK. Most of us ended up bumping into each other while wandering around looking for our objectives and just ended up hanging out for a while, out of sight of the instructors. They gave us so many objectives that there was no way we could find them all in the allotted time anyway. The nighttime one was miserable. We weren't supposed to use flashlights, so we ended up blindly tearing through the brush to try and find our objectives. When Sherman and I became disoriented, we stumbled across Sergeant Moose who directed us up a steep embankment. By the time we got to the top, crawling half the way, I was drenched in sweat. We sat to catch our breath and I drifted off to sleep while looking at the lights of the big houses on the nearby hills. I don't think we found more than a couple of the objectives, and barely made our way back to the classroom by the drop-dead time.

The one piece of training that I'm really looking forward to is the IED class. It's been repeated over and over that IEDs are the deadliest weapon we'll likely face in Iraq. Frankly, I don't think we really know much about them, at least in terms of the best ways to spot or avoid them. The instructors have also been emphasizing the difficulty of the IED course that we'll be doing later in the training cycle. Apparently, it's a training simulation where we will patrol through an area and have to react to an IED attack. It sounds like good training, probably something we should do more than once.

San Mateo, Camp Pendleton, CA
July 25, 2004

I shouldn't go so long without writing. So this will probably be another long entry as a lot has happened since the last time I wrote. We had a change of pace from the routine we'd fallen into and were loaded onto buses to head to March AFB (Air Force Base) for a week of SASO (Security and Stability Operations) training with the infantry battalion we'll be supporting. March AFB is an old, decommissioned air base a couple hours away. We set up in an empty town of sorts— the old and abandoned base housing. Things didn't start out well. The day we arrived, before we had started any training, a guy from one of the other units died in a vehicle accident. We had been killing time in one of the abandoned houses, since the training exercises didn't start until the next day. Meanwhile, all the drivers had to report for driver training to practice J-turns. I'd never heard of it before, but apparently a J-turn is a driving move to react to enemy contact where you turn sharply to get out of the line of fire. While practicing, a Humvee flipped over and killed one of the guys inside. I heard that it was the guy in the turret that was killed, but I don't know for sure. If so, it seems stupid to practice dangerous driving maneuvers with a guy in the turret, or even with the turret open—a potential accident waiting to happen. Because of the accident, the SASO training exercise was delayed for a day for a "safety stand-down." The evening of the first full day, we held a memorial service for the guy who was killed. I obviously didn't know him since he was from a different unit, but I feel terrible for his family. It would be one thing to be killed or lose a loved one in Iraq, even to an accident. But, for whatever reason, when something like this happens in training in California, it's just not the same. To be sure, whether it's in Cali or Iraq, it's obviously still a sacrifice for your country. But I think if it's going to happen, everyone I know would prefer to go down in a blaze of glory, taking out bad guys, not to an accident stateside. Besides, things like that really shouldn't happen here.

During the safety stand-down day, we learned a little more about what the upcoming training was going to be like. There were to be a few classes on the first day, followed by practical application in a "real-life" training exercise. We were conducting the exercise with an infantry battalion. Each of the three infantry companies in the battalion was given a "base" in the abandoned town to run missions out of—sort of a mock war with the instructors acting as Iraqis. It ended up being good training. Once the exercise finally started, our platoon was split up by squads, each going to support a different infantry company. This was the day we, or at least I, had been dreading. It's what is going to happen once we finally deploy, and I hope our experience at March AFB doesn't serve as a preview of what is to come. We are a pretty tight platoon and we know how to do our job, so to be divvied out and integrated into the infantry companies was hard. I guess I can understand the grunts' perspective, they had a "we don't know you, don't get in our way" type of approach. It's frustrating from our point of view. They view us as extra bodies that they can stick with the shittiest duties. I know it'll take some time to prove ourselves, but I'm not looking forward to it.

We're being deployed with the 1st Battalion, 23rd Marines (1/23), a reserve infantry battalion from Texas. Initially, our squad was assigned to support "Carlos" company—jokingly called that instead of "Charlie" because it's almost entirely made up of Hispanics. We heard that one of their platoons can only speak Spanish. We were only attached to them for the first day but based on what I saw, it confirmed in my mind the rumor that they are the best company in the battalion. They're disciplined, professional, and seem to have good NCOs. At first, we were worried because they wanted us to fortify their base instead of going to the classes with them, but luckily the SSgts came by to save us. Not a great start, but I don't think they realized that we will actually be joining them in Iraq and weren't there to just help with the SASO training. After that, they were very professional and treated us just the same as their own. They seemed to have a large number of guys that were previously active duty, so they likely have a good sense of how to use their engineers. Still, we are all nervous to see how the grunts will end up using us in operations when we actually get in-country. We could either be left behind on every major mission and be bored to death for the next seven months, or they could do the opposite, and use us in the worst situations in lieu of their own guys. My hope is that it's somewhere in between and that we're used in the kind of missions that we've been trained to do.

After that first day, our squad was separated from Carlos and attached to Alpha. Alpha Company is made up of guys from Houston. They seemed a little less disciplined than Carlos, but their NCOs left a generally good impression. Both units had much newer gear than our own. Maybe I've seen too many movies, but I half expected the grunts to be better than us in every way. Marine Corps infantry has a well-earned reputation. That said, they were more or less the same, with similar levels of experience and discipline. The early part of the live training was spent doing patrols around the "town" and sweeping for IEDs. At one point, we called out when we thought we'd sighted a potential IED in a pile of garbage with wires sticking out of it. We took cover and sat around for a half hour in the sun while we waited for "EOD" (Explosive Ordnance Disposal) to arrive. EOD ended up being an instructor who eventually walked up and told us that it wasn't an IED, and to keep moving. In general, the early part of the training wasn't too dissimilar to what we had been doing in San Mateo, with the exception of being integrated with the grunts.

We went through the final field exercise, the "fake war," on the last day with Alpha. It served as the wrap-up to the training, with no more guidance from the instructors. We ran a lot of patrols and IED drills and, all in all, it was pretty decent training. Using paint rounds instead of blanks would have made it more realistic, but other than that, the instructors made every effort to simulate real combat. They even played the daily prayers from the "mosques." We were "mortared" at night by the instructors occasionally lobbing training grenades into our base, so sleep was pretty sporadic. For the final exercise, we went on a nine-hour night patrol. I was a little disappointed with what I saw of the grunts on patrol. They were falling asleep and talking loudly in the house where we had set up our OP (Observation Post) for the night, so not exactly stealthy. I was with a group led by one of their Gunnery Sergeants and, when some of the insurgent role players moved into our field of fire, instead of firing, he ran out of the house to try and capture them. It seemed so stupid, or at least unrealistic, considering they were all carrying AKs. Hopefully, he just wasn't taking the training seriously and that wasn't something he would really do over there. Either way, I hope I'm not around him much—he seemed like a dick.

The last day of the training program was dedicated to cleaning up. I'm still not sure I understand the point, as we were in an abandoned town simulating a war-torn Iraqi city. We were also told that, after one more training cycle, the place was going to be demolished. Instead of cleaning, I wandered around with Weaver, Burdette, and a few of the guys and smashed up the insides of the houses, breaking mirrors and kicking holes in walls. It seemed like a good way to waste the day—at least it was much more fun. We were all happy to join back up with the rest of the platoon that afternoon. It's funny, we were only gone from each other for a few days, but you could sense everyone's relief at being back together. While we waited for the bus, the SSgts went out and got a bunch of burgers and it almost felt like a celebration of sorts. We had a faux-bodybuilding competition—Burdette won by putting on his shades and sticking out his gut while he flexed and contorted in awkward positions. Swinney was a close runner up.

Today was our second day back in the classroom at San Mateo. I had gotten poison sumac while doing the land navigation training and it's finally started to clear up. It made the time at March AFB miserable. It was so hot and we were moving around so much, the rash was in a constant state of irritation. We did engineer recon training classes yesterday and practiced application today. It primarily consists of assessing the strength of bridges or the depth of a river ford, stuff like that. Again, nothing really new or probably very useful. The word seems to change on a daily basis as to when we'll be leaving. It now looks like there will be no advanced party, so I won't get to go early. Instead, the entire unit will ship out on the sixteenth of August—a little sooner than expected. You would think that they should know when we will be leaving from the very moment we received the mobilization order. They must know which unit we're replacing and when that unit is scheduled to come home.

In any case, the rumor is that we'll be deploying to somewhere near the Syrian border. Apparently, it's an extremely dangerous place due to the high number of foreign fighters that cross into Iraq from both Syria and Jordan. I'm not sure where it started, but everyone has been quoting the figure that one in every three convoys is ambushed or hit by an IED in the area. That figure seems too high to me given the number of daily casualties, but I suppose it all depends on the number of convoys per day and the likelihood of someone being killed or wounded in each attack. Apparently, Carlos from 1/23 has sent over an advanced party, which has already seen some action, so maybe it is realistic. It's difficult to estimate how much fighting goes on over there from the casualty figures alone. There could be only one casualty per ten IED attacks, or maybe it's one per hundred—I have no idea. No one I've talked to knows either but, depending on what that figure is, it could give us a good idea of just how much action we're likely to see in our area. The rundown, as it stands today, is that Carlos will be going to the city of Hit along the Euphrates and will be the battalion's "go-to" company when things get hot. Alpha is going to a city along the Syrian border, which doesn't sound like it will be much better. While

Bravo is going to be guarding Haditha Dam on the Euphrates. We don't know which of our squads will be going with each infantry company, but I'm willing to bet that we go with Alpha since that's the unit we did the SASO training alongside.

One bit of good news. We were told that if the grunts aren't using us properly after thirty days in-country, then they'll pull our whole platoon back together, making us a part of 1/23's headquarters unit and only dishing us out on missions on an as-needed basis. I have my doubts as to whether that will actually happen, whether we're used appropriately or not, but at least it's something to hope for. As a last resort, Captain Kuniholm can use it as a threat to make sure that they at least try to use us somewhat appropriately. It also looks like I might get my fireteam back, because GG may be joining the new 4th squad that's being formed. While that would be good, I really wish all this reshuffling would have been settled before we started the pre-deployment training.

It struck me today that by this time next month, we'll be in Iraq. I'm not sure that I feel much more prepared than I did at this time a month ago. Now that things are getting closer, I'm starting to get a little more nervous. Perhaps nervous isn't the right word; it's more of a combination of both nerves and excitement. A mixture of fear, anticipation, excitement, and genuinely not looking forward to months of extremely hard and tedious work. Although, God knows, hard work may be the least of my worries. I think what I may be looking forward to the least is when a patrol or raid that I'm *not* involved in gets hit. It's going to be more stressful than actually being part of the group that's getting hit, just in a different way. To hear that some of our guys are in action while we can only sit around base and wait to hear the results will be a painful experience. I'm also nervous to know how I'll perform in action. They always say that you never know how you're going to react until things actually kick off. The hardest guy in the platoon could fall into a crying mess after the first shots, while the biggest slacker may kick ass. It's a weird feeling—to know that there is a very high likelihood that within the next couple months, for the first and hopefully last time in my life, someone will be shooting at me. Or worse, setting off a bomb right next to me. I suppose it shouldn't really feel weird. After all, I'm in the Marine Corps during a time of war. It probably has more to do with the fact that, just a couple months ago, it seemed like such a remote possibility. I was probably a bit naïve about my chances of being called up. Despite being in the Reserves, I felt just like any other college kid. But whereas everyone else's next few months will bring a return to school to study and party, my future has taken a very different turn. Active duty units don't really have to make the same huge mental adjustment when they get deployed. For us, it's a big and—hopefully, for our sakes—very quick transition. I think we're doing a pretty good job.

But despite all the training and mental preparation, there's no way to know how I'll react in actual combat. I feel confident now, but when shit actually hits the fan, the fear will be intense; hopefully the adrenaline will overcome it. I don't want to let my friends down and, perhaps selfishly, I don't want to let myself down. I wouldn't be able to live with it, to go through life knowing, deep down, that I'm a coward. It's very surreal to contemplate death at age twenty-two. My life can be quickly dashed away in a moment by some uneducated dickhead with an AK and a chip on his shoulder. All the time people have spent with me—from swim lessons as a kid to college classes—would be for nothing. Just pink mist and a memory, as they say. I know that I'm no more special in the grand scheme of things than the myriad Iraqis that we've killed. All of us are just pieces of a larger geopolitical game, no different than any warrior throughout history. But still, after everything that's gone into making me who I am, I hate to think that my story may end as just another name on a casualty list.

Well, I've caught up on everything. It's now late and everyone else is asleep. I've got to write more often so I don't have to do these marathon sessions.

San Mateo, Camp Pendleton, CA
July 26, 2004

A bit of good news—home leave has been confirmed for the second through the tenth of August, much longer than we'd expected. Burdette, Miles, Miller, Weaver, myself and a couple others plan on going to Vegas. Hopefully it doesn't change and nobody backs out—I'd like some stories to reminisce about over the next seven months.

We trained on demolitions today and will go to the range tomorrow to blow some stuff up. A lot of the training covered topics that we've all seen before, but it's always good to run through them again, especially since these are the skills we'll most likely use over there. We went through the different demolition charges used for urban breaching—shots for blowing down doors or holes in walls to support raids. Cool stuff, but somehow they still manage to find a way to make it boring and tedious. Perhaps it's the long days catching up with us; everyone has been having a hard time staying awake in class. Up early every day for PT followed by classes all day long, only pausing for meals. I have to hand it to the instructors, they pull some pretty long days.

I'm feeling a little more upbeat today. Reading through my last entry, I seemed to be in a funk. The days go in ups and downs. I'm probably a little fatigued like everyone else. At least we now have home leave to look forward to, but I'm still anxious to just get the show on the road. Like most things, once we get into it, all the fear and anticipation will melt away and we can get into a routine. Or, if not a routine, at least get to the point where we have some idea of what the future holds for us. Right now, I really have no idea what Iraq will be like, and the anticipation is killing me. After a couple months in-country, things will likely just tick along. At the very least, there will be a war to keep things interesting.

San Mateo, Camp Pendleton, CA
July 27, 2004

We went to the demo range this morning and did some of the urban breaching shots we'd reviewed in the classroom yesterday. We also did some regular shots—steel cutting, wire breaching, and a couple others. The urban stuff was good, because we had to stand at the minimum standoff distance like we will in an actual raid. We've practiced the standoff calculations before but haven't actually been that close to the shot. It's amazing how even a little charge, set to blow off a door handle, will ring your bell when you're only eight to ten feet away. The range had door frames set up with plywood doors attached; we'd set off the shot then rush through the door afterwards. I was the breacher who set up one of the charges. When I stomped down on the igniter, it tilted to the side in the dirt and didn't blow. All the guys not on the breach team were waiting and listening to the countdown for the shot to go off to take pictures of the blast. They all clicked their pictures at the end of the countdown but, because I had to stomp on it again, all they got was a picture of a plywood board hanging on a doorframe—kind of funny.

We only have a few days left at Camp Pendleton. We've started into the final classes on IEDs, a final review of foreign mines, and how to deal with UXO (Unexploded Ordnance). These are probably some of the classes that we will rely on the most, though it still seems to be up for debate as to whether engineers should be dealing with unexploded ordnance. Landmines are a no brainer, but depending on the type of UXO, it can be pretty unstable and we aren't trained on how to identify all the various types. I think when it comes to it, it'll just be a judgment call. Apparently, some infantry units have also been using their engineers to take care of IEDs since there aren't enough EOD teams in Iraq, but we're definitely not trained for that.

We've been told that we're going to do the IED course on Friday, which is supposed to be intense. The IED class this afternoon scared the shit out of everyone. The instructor who lost his eye to a landmine in the invasion showed us videos of attacks and ambushes in Iraq that the insurgents have posted online. He's a good instructor and didn't pull any punches, emphasizing the fact that we will almost never see an attack coming. All we can do is wait for the IED to go off, then try to pull ourselves together to properly react by hunting down and killing the triggerman. He added the caveat that it is almost impossible to find the guys who set off the IEDs—so yeah, I'm not feeling too pumped about that prospect. One of the videos showed an IED hit a vehicle. Then, as a bunch of guys ran up to the vehicle to assist with the wounded, a secondary IED went off. It makes me both angry and anxious—it's such a cowardly way to fight. Initially, most of the IEDs in Iraq were set off with electrical wire strung directly from the triggerman to the charge. But the insurgents are increasingly using wireless IEDs, so it's now even more difficult to locate the triggerman, since wireless IEDs give them more standoff distance and don't have a wire leading from the bomb directly to them. Basically, by the time it goes off, they will most likely be driving away while we're still scrambling to react and see if there are any casualties. Unfortunately, the attacks of this nature are only getting more sophisticated. They change to adapt to our tactics as fast as we change to adapt to them, a never-ending cycle that makes for a more dangerous battlefield.

Everyone is looking forward to home leave. A lot of guys are going home for the entire week, but I would prefer to avoid going through the good-byes again. A week at home would be surreal at this point anyway; I feel like I've already detached myself from it all. It's times like this when I'm glad that I don't have a wife and kids. I'm already in the right frame of mind, a week at home would throw things out of whack. I already feel separated from my friends and family. Although it's been less than a month, the knowledge of what is coming my way puts a great distance between myself and everyone at home. If I survive and return home intact, I'm a little worried how this may change me. It may just be paranoia brought on from the classes they've given us on post-traumatic stress, but I don't think anyone knows in advance how they'll respond to this kind of mental trauma. It all really depends on what we experience over there. Some guys go over and see almost no action, while some are getting hit every other day. I've told myself that I'll only change as much as I allow myself—that it's all within my control. The truth is that it probably isn't. I guess that's why there are no atheists in foxholes, why everyone in war is a causality, and all the other clichés that get bandied about. It must not be too terrible if so many guys join up with contractors to go back over, although the healthy paycheck can't hurt.

I feel like I can really relate to the "duality of man" philosophy mentioned in *Full Metal Jacket*. I both want and don't want to kill anyone. Just like I both want and don't want to see much combat. Selfishly, I hope I don't kill anyone, simply because I don't want that potential mental burden for the rest of my life. At this point in my life, I don't really think it would be an issue, but I have no way of knowing. Down the road, it may be something that bothers me and, if given the choice, I'd rather not. The fact is that I won't have a choice and may end up killing someone who is simply fighting to expel what they see as a foreign invader. I can't really fault them for that and would probably be doing the same if the roles were reversed. I don't have any animosity towards regular Iraqis, or even the regular Iraqi military. On the other hand, although it may seem callous, it would be exciting to get a kill. I've tried to understand why that is. Possibly, I want to experience what warriors have experienced for centuries. I guess it's similar to why people climb Everest: to do something that not many people have the desire or ability to do. I also think it would provide some kind of mental security. If I do end up being killed, I'd like to know that I took one of them with me.

Whether we see much action or not, it's going to be a long seven months. Initially, I thought so primarily because of the type of conditions that we'll be living in but, as our departure date grows closer, so does the real fear and concern about what is to come. It's all the unknowns. In my life thus far, I may not have always known exactly what was going to happen over the next seven months, but I've usually had a pretty good idea. The one thing that I do know is that I'll never be the same after this. If this was World War II and we were fighting to defend ourselves, I may not have these kinds of misgivings. Instead, as a professional fighting force, we're just going where they tell us to go and fighting who they tell us to fight, because that's what we've signed up to do. There's no discussion amongst the guys about any kind of national cause. In fact, I haven't heard anyone mention it even once. I'm sure it was probably different with Afghanistan; we went there because we were attacked. But Iraq must be a somewhat new event in the history of warfare—going to war without a real geopolitical objective. I guess we have the nominal objective of protecting ourselves from WMDs, but even that's not really valid anymore. I guess we can't just say, "sorry, our bad," and pull out. Instead, we have to keep going with a war that now lacks a catalyst or cause. It would almost be comical if it weren't so sad. I'm a little confused as to how Iraq became an issue in the first place; it seemed to come out of nowhere. It went from rarely being in the news, to suddenly being the primary topic of discussion without any real reason that I can discern. All of a sudden people were talking about invasion, and I still don't know how the situation changed in Iraq versus a few years ago when it was a non-issue.

In any case, I can't be too aggrieved—I signed up for this. At this point, I'm just taking it one week at a time. I'm looking forward to one last week of normal life, then back to 29 Palms on the tenth with the expectation that we'll finally ship out on the sixteenth.

San Mateo, Camp Pendleton, CA
July 28, 2004

Today, we had more classes on weapons (50 cal., MK19, SAW, SMAW, and M240G), then practicing radio reports (FLASH, SPOT and Medical Evacuations). All stuff that we've practiced quite a bit before. It was pretty clear that they didn't have anything in particular scheduled for today. In a couple days, we'll be going to 29 Palms and then, hopefully, we'll be released for home leave that evening. I don't think we'll be leaving for Vegas until the second, because we'll get to 29 Palms too late to rent a car.

San Mateo, Camp Pendleton, CA
July 29, 2004

Today started off fine, with some more weapons classes and mock gun drills. Again, nothing really new, but probably not a bad thing to review again. We had to make shooting noises as the instructor called out mock "targets" to our left and right, while we would quickly adjust our "fire." I spent most the time laughing at the way Miles was making absurd sounds, partly "machine gun" sounds mixed in with some imitation screaming.

After a quick lunch, we finally went to do the IED course that we've heard so much about. To throw a twist into things, all the senior NCOs from our platoon were separated from our group to join in a live-fire M203 shoot at a different location. This left Strong and Burdette in charge of the platoon; I don't think either was too thrilled. We've been told about the difficulty of this course from day one, so to throw the junior NCOs into the fire without any warning left everyone a bit nonplussed. I suppose it could be viewed as an opportunity to step up, but this required fire-team leaders to step up to the platoon leader level— a tall order.

We had very little time to prep, so things started off as a bit of a cluster right off the bat. We were supposed to go on "patrol" around the area, pretending not to know where an IED may explode but maintaining an alert stance and being on the lookout. Early in the patrol, the instructors messed with our radios so we had to use hand and arm signals, which caused some added confusion. I felt bad for Strong and Burdette—not only is it difficult to go from being fire-team leaders to commanding the entire platoon, but all the instructors were eying and critiquing their every move, waiting to jump on them whenever there was a screw up. We were stopped by the instructors at one point and told that we were doing a shitty job of patrolling and had to start back at the beginning. In retrospect, I think this was just because they didn't have the IED section of the course set up yet. In any case, we started over again and were guided by the instructors to a certain area where the "IEDs" were obviously located. The "attack" was supposed to come as a surprise and catch us off guard, but the area was cordoned off with safety tape and a large group of instructors were milling around. Even though we were all prepared and alert, since we knew the "IEDs" would be going off any minute, once we were hit, things immediately fell apart. The "IEDs" were just instructors throwing popping grenades. They went off up and down the entire platoon, rather than just one, which is what we had expected. Then, before we had time to react, a guy dressed as a suicide bomber rushed at us, which was quickly followed by a "mortar" attack (more popping grenades). The instructors ran around tapping people as either being "dead" or "wounded," with over half the platoon down in the first couple minutes.

I couldn't help but roll my eyes. If over half the platoon is dead or wounded in less than a minute, then we're probably pretty well screwed and our only hope would be to hunker down and call for help. I'm not sure what this exercise in extremes was supposed to teach us. The course was designed as a worst-case scenario, which is fine. But it was so ludicrous that it went beyond the point of being useful. We ran around, trying to drag the wounded back and set up some kind of defensive perimeter while calling in support and medevacs. I'm not sure what else could be expected of us but, for whatever reason, the instructors went absolutely berserk. They stopped everything and told us we had done a shitty job—the worst that they'd ever seen. We were told that we had to start over and do it again. The second time didn't go much better, or at least we didn't do anything different. In the second round, I was tapped as "dead" in the first set of attacks. I can understand the benefit of training for the worst-case scenario but there's also some benefit, arguably more benefit, of training for the most likely scenarios. Not the situations where an entire platoon is pinned down and taking over 50% casualties in two minutes, but the situations where we are hit by one or two IEDs followed by some small-arms fire. Of course, the counterargument is that if we can handle the worst-case scenario, then everything else will be easy, but it just doesn't work like that. At this point, I still don't really know how we're supposed to respond to a single IED hitting a convoy and, odds are, that's what I'm most likely to see over there.

What really pissed me, and everyone else, off the most was that after our senior NCOs returned from the M203 shoot, the instructors told them that we had done horribly. SSgt Dreany talked to us under the pavilion next to the barracks for a solid hour, berating us for our poor performance. He focused most of his attention on the NCOs, taking all of the corporal's chevrons and throwing them out. I'm positive that if they had been there to see how ludicrous the course was, they wouldn't have thought twice about it, nor would they have done any better. We were set up to fail. He went around asking each of the NCOs what we had done in each of the two times that we went through the course. I told him I helped collect casualties while setting up a perimeter on the first, and "died" right away in the second. I wanted to ask what he would have done differently, but it definitely wasn't the right time—it was a pretty tense atmosphere. I could see Burdette was steaming while Strong was, as always, calm. But no one was happy about it. I'm not sure what the SSgt's motivation was for his tirade. Sometimes, he puts on a bit of a show to drive home a point, but this time he seemed genuinely pissed. To single out the junior NCOs and embarrass us in front of the rest of the platoon does nothing for morale or to develop our leadership abilities. He can't knock us down in front of everyone and then expect them to listen to us tomorrow.

At any rate, this pretty much finishes our training at Camp Pendleton. Not exactly a high point to go out on, but at least we're moving on to the next step in this process. I'm still a little bitter about the way things ended but am taking it in stride, which probably wouldn't be the case if I were one of the main guys that had been singled out. We head to 29 Palms in a day or two and then should get home leave. It can't come soon enough.

29 Palms, CA
August 10, 2004

Yet again, I've been remiss in my writing and have to catch up. The last couple of days at Camp Pendleton went pretty quickly. We inventoried our gear, cleaned our rifles, and got ready to move to 29 Palms—nothing too exciting. While cleaning rifles, I jokingly leaned against the wall and let water dribble out of my camelback in front of me so, from behind, it looked like I was taking a leak on the side of the building. I even let out a little groan of relief. The guys around me laughed but Captain Kuniholm saw it and thought it was for real. As I turned around, he was just about to lay into me before he saw that it was a joke—pretty funny, and he took it in good humor. We arrived in 29 Palms the evening of the second. I haven't been here since my first summer AT (Advanced Training) with the unit back in 2002: still a shithole in the middle of nowhere, same as before. We were given leave until the tenth, which we were only able to get because we are now officially attached to 1/23, who had been granted a week of leave. They've been mobilized longer than us, so it makes sense for them to get some leave but I don't think the other platoons in our company get it, so it was a lucky coincidence for us.

Those of us who went to Vegas didn't leave until the evening of the third. It's hard to describe, and seems silly in retrospect, but being stuck on base just one day longer than the rest of the platoon sent us all into a frenzy. We just wanted to get out of there as quick as we could in order to not waste another minute of our leave in 29 Palms. We were stuck after everyone else had left, because all of the platoon's gear had been left in the unlocked barracks building, and until the lock could be fixed, it had to be guarded. Everyone else was already gone while we were still trying to sort out rental cars, so we were stuck with the job. We decided to move all the gear to a different building that had a lock, which took a couple hours of running the eighty-odd sea bags and packs back and forth in the hot summer sun. As it turns out, we weren't allowed to move the gear to that building, so we had to move everything back. All of this in the August heat of the Mojave Desert. Eventually, the lock of the door in the original building was fixed and we were finally allowed to leave. It was worth it, getting out of there was the best feeling. The first day of a vacation is always the best; you've got the whole trip to look forward to. Any thoughts of Iraq seemed like a long ways away. Even though training had really only been for a few weeks, it had been an intense time. It felt like we had been pent-up and were finally set loose. Driving the beat-up rental car to Vegas was awesome. The combination of the wide-open desert highway and the knowledge that this would be our last taste of freedom was indescribable. I drove the hell out of that rental car, gunning it the whole way. We eventually had to exchange it in Vegas for another after it finally died on us.

Burdette, Miles, Weaver, James, Miller and myself went in two cars. We had a great time. Miles got pick-pocketed by a prostitute, who accosted him while we were walking home one night. We all lost a lot of money, ate too much, went to a club and a show, and drank as much as we possibly could. Towards the end of the week, I ended up flying home after all. It was just a couple days and wasn't planned in advance, but I'm glad I did. Mom called while I was in Vegas and was pretty upset. She felt that she had given me the impression that she didn't want me to come home. In truth, I did get that impression—I thought she didn't want to go through the good-byes again. It turns out that she just didn't want me to feel pressured to come home. Still, it was nice to squeeze in one last visit. I went fishing and spent some time with the family. The good-byes weren't too bad this time around. On the first leg of the flight back to Vegas, I was able to sit with Dad since he was heading out on a business trip. It was kind of awkward to part ways in the airport. Even though it was a significant, emotional moment, between all the hustle and bustle and need to get to our connecting flights, we just quickly said good-bye and parted ways.

I flew back into Vegas on Monday evening. As I was walking through the airport, I heard someone yell, "Hey, devil dog!" in that tone that sounds like you're about to get chewed out by a drill instructor. I'm so conditioned that, for a split second, I thought "shit, what have I done wrong," before I realized that I was in civilian clothes and in an airport where no one should know me. It turned out to be Strong, coming back from visiting his family in Vermont. We shared a cab to the hotel and met up with everyone for our last night out. It was kind of funny—it turns out the cab driver had been stationed at San Mateo before he shipped out for Vietnam. Small world. It was good having Strong there for the last night. Even though he doesn't drink or gamble, he's a lot of fun. As I drank more, I started losing more and more money. Strong would offer his "recommendation" on how I should bet by either nodding or shaking his head in a very solemn manner. Since I could barely see straight by the end, I followed what he said blindly. It probably saved me a lot of money. We were a wreck that last night. I demanded a free breakfast from the pit boss, which they gave us. Weaver broke a glass that the waitress was handing him and made a scene in the lobby because an ATM ate his card, which was probably a blessing in disguise. In all, the night was a disaster—exactly what we needed. We walked out of the MGM Grand at 0700, covering our eyes from the bright sun. Good times.

On the way back to 29 Palms we swung by the Hoover Dam, which for whatever reason didn't really impress me much. I suppose I just wasn't in the right frame of mind to enjoy it. Eating at the Subway on base tonight was one of the most depressing meals of my life. Up until now, we've always had the hope of home leave to look forward to and, once leave was confirmed, we had the anticipation of hitting Vegas with the boys. We could avoid thinking about the brutal months ahead by knowing that we would have this time off. Really, there's always been something next in the progression towards deployment—SASO training at March AFB, then the IED course, then home leave. Now, the only thing left to do is get on the plane and go; it's both scary and exciting. On a somewhat funny note, it's crazy to hear how much trouble some of these guys can get into with just one week off. I heard that Johnson got arrested while on leave. Apparently he was drunk and wrecked his rental car. The judge let him go because of the deployment, but he's going to have to serve time when he gets home since this was his second DUI—crazy bastard. Also, Killsbury got into a car wreck and won't be deploying due to his injury. One of the guys that joined our platoon right before we were activated didn't show back up today, so we're guessing he's made a run for it. Good thing leave didn't last a week longer, or we might not have much of a platoon left to deploy.

29 Palms, CA
August 11, 2004

This morning, the SSgts took us on a long trail run into the desert bordering the main section of base. The sun was rising as we ran. It can actually be a beautiful place at that time of day, before the heat gets too brutal. The knowledge that we're finally on the home stretch seemed to hit me as we ran. That, combined with the feeling of running through such a wide-open expanse, was an exhilarating feeling. If I would have been told just a few months ago that I'd be spending a morning this August running in the Mojave Desert, watching the sun rise, I wouldn't have believed you. There's a kind of freedom in not having control over your own life.

Unfortunately, one of the biggest downsides to this place also became apparent as we ran. We all had to dodge a rattlesnake that was sitting in the middle of the trail. By the end of the run, a good number of guys couldn't keep up with the pace the SSgts had set—a little too much boozing during leave. Afterwards, SSgt Dreany went on a rant about how we're not physically or mentally prepared for what's to come, but that it's too late to do anything about it, which killed my reflective state of mind. It's also probably not what the platoon really needs to hear at this point, regardless of whether it's true or not. Less than two months isn't a long time to get ready for a war, even though, in theory, we could be deployed without any ramp-up training at all. If this experience has taught me anything thus far, it's that the use of part-time military units isn't suitable for every type of conflict. Boot camp really only teaches discipline and instills a sense of the Marine Corps history and culture. Our infantry training is decent but brief, and has been scaled back to the point where we learn a little about a whole lot of subjects. Our MOS training was pretty thorough and probably the only training that was really worth the time. Typically, you continue to learn after you've joined your active-duty unit but for Reservists, I don't think one weekend a month and two weeks in the summer can always cut it. Modern warfare is too complex of an environment. For a country that's as sensitive to casualties as the U.S., and is involved in two asymmetric conflicts, Reserve units are being asked to carry a heavy burden.

Pre-Deployment Iraq

At the time of Charlie Company's deployment, the situation in Iraq was growing more dangerous and unstable by the day. The general public had seemingly only recently become aware of the fact that the situation had taken a turn for the worse following the immediate success of the invasion. By late-2003 into early-2004, the resistance to Coalition forces had shifted from the organized Iraqi Army and Fedayeen units faced in the invasion to numerous disparate insurgent groups composed of a broad spectrum of fighters with varying ideologies and objectives. As Charlie Company prepared to deploy, these insurgent groups began to reach a higher state of operational efficiency, having had the time necessary to organize and test their mettle in the early months of the occupation. The most lethal insurgent groups were beginning to receive significant contributions, in both money and recruits, from outside of Iraq. Fragmented between ex-Baathists, disenfranchised Sunnis, fanatical foreign fighters, local Sunni and Shiite militia groups, and nationalists who simply wanted to rid their country of foreign invaders—these insurgent groups were accelerating both the number and level of sophistication of their attacks. Meanwhile, the U.S. military was scrambling to adapt to the changing battlefield and the enemy's tactics and weaponry.

Al-Qaeda in Iraq (AQI) had made its brutal, prime-time debut to the world in May 2004 with the beheading of Nicholas Berg by the group's leader, Abu Musab al-Zarqawi. Meanwhile, other predominantly Sunni insurgent groups had been formed with the dual objectives of both attacking Coalition troops and stoking sectarian strife by attacking the Shiite populace. Perhaps surprisingly to many Americans, the Shiite population that had suffered greatly under the leadership of Saddam Hussein and had been counted on to support the occupation, also began actively attacking Coalition forces. Largely spearheaded by Muqtada Al Sadr's Mahdi Army, attacks across all major Shiite population centers tied down thousands of Coalition troops, which had otherwise been expected to deploy to Sunni-dominated areas. Authority over the country had only recently been passed from the U.S. led Coalition Provisional Authority (CPA) to the Iraqi Interim Government; however, this interim government had been formed under the supervision of the Coalition and, for that reason alone, held little sway over the general populace and next to no control in openly hostile majority Sunni areas such as Al Anbar province.

Meanwhile recent setbacks such as the ambushing of a Blackwater convoy in Fallujah in March 2004, followed by the subsequent aborted attempt to pacify the city in April 2004 underscored the fact that the mission was far from accomplished. In short, the country was in total disarray. There was no central authority and most cities or neighborhoods were controlled by local insurgent groups which often focused on criminal enterprises, such as extortion or kidnapping, as much as the war against the occupiers. It was into this maelstrom that U.S. and Coalition troops were deploying in mid–2004. The main area of deployment for Marine Corps units was the western Iraqi province of Al Anbar—the heartland of the Sunni insurgency. Al Anbar includes cities that now hold a place in Marine Corps history such as Fallujah, Al-Qaim, Hit, Haditha, and the provincial capital of Ramadi.

The day our platoon had been dreading eventually came to pass as we were separated from each other, with each individual squad being assigned to support various infantry companies. Second Squad, to which I belonged, was to be sent to a totally different area of the country from the remainder of the platoon. We were ordered to support the Marines of Alpha Company, 1st Battalion, 23rd Marine Regiment, a Reserve infantry company based in Houston, Texas, which was being stationed at Forward Operating Base (FOB) Korean Village, also known as Camp KV or simply KV. Located near the Syrian and Jordanian borders, roughly thirty minutes west of the city of Ar Rutbah, Camp KV had previously been a small village located alongside the highway. The village was built to provide housing for the construction workers employed in the highway's development; however, it had since been

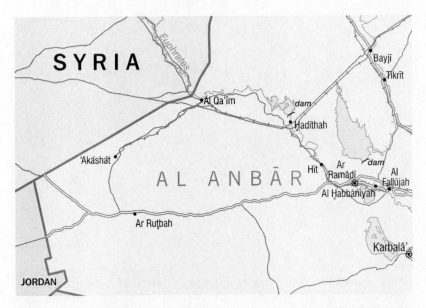

A view of western Iraq. The Marines of Camp KV were responsible for an area of operations which encompassed the border crossing of Trebil on the Jordanian border and Al Walid on the Syrian border, as well as the Iraqi cities of Akashat and Ar Rutbah.

abandoned before being occupied by the U.S. military. Once integrated into Alpha Company at Camp KV, we operated alongside a company from the 3rd Light Armored Reconnaissance (LAR) battalion. Operations included manning the two border crossings, patrolling and conducting raids in the city of Ar Rutbah and its outlying villages, and maintaining security on Route Mobile—the main highway from Syria and Jordan that runs all the way to Ramadi. Ensuring the security of Routes Mobile and Michigan, a secondary supply route that parallels Mobile, was our paramount mission as miles-long supply convoys used these routes to bring supplies from Jordan to Coalition bases located in the heart of the country.

The nearest Iraqi city of Ar Rutbah is predominantly Sunni, with an estimated population of anywhere from 25,000 to 55,000. A maze of tightly packed houses and winding streets and alleys, it's nearly impossible to estimate the population with any accuracy—particularly as one household can often contain more than a dozen people. The

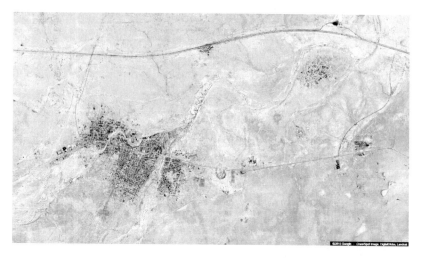

An aerial view of Ar Rutbah and surroundings, and our main operating areas around the city. Route Mobile, to the north of the city, runs east-west from the Jordanian and Syrian borders to Ar Ramadi. Route Michigan runs parallel, passing directly through Ar Rutbah. These roads are connected by Route Phoenix, running north-south on the western edge of the city (Cnes/Spot Image 2015).

city holds many tribal ties to the major family clans in Fallujah and frequently served as a safe haven for fighters from that city, in the event that things became too hot for them at home. In addition, its location near the joint border crossings made it strategically important as it proved to be the ideal place for foreign fighters to rendezvous before making their way to join insurgent groups deeper in Iraq. The local population was largely opposed to the U.S. presence and was particularly aggrieved by the accidental bombing of the city's hospital during the 2003 invasion. The primary source of the populace's anger with the U.S., however, seemed to stem more from economic, rather than political, reasons. Specifically, the U.S. presence disrupted the city's chief economic activity—smuggling. Prior to the war, smuggling was the primary occupation of a large portion of the city's population and, based on the palatial size of some of the homes in the city, appears to have been extremely lucrative. Everything from food to cigarettes was smuggled in order to avoid taxes and tariffs, making a fortune for the most efficient and well connected operators.

After several weeks of running operations out of Camp KV, the area commanders settled on an allocation of force composed of two teams formed by a combination of the LAR Company and the infantry of Alpha Company. Each team was composed of one infantry platoon and one LAR platoon, which were to work jointly to conduct operations in the area. Meanwhile, the remaining Marines of both companies were either sent to man the border crossings or guard the perimeter of Camp KV. One team typically conducted operations in and around the city for several days by patrolling, setting up observation posts (OPs), raiding target houses, and manning vehicle checkpoints; while the other would remain at Camp KV to rest and act as a reactionary force in case of emergency. To support each of the teams, our combat engineer squad was also split into two groups and integrated into each of the teams.

Fire-Team Two, the one to which I belonged, quickly formed a tight bond—both operationally and personally. Of course we had known each other prior to the deployment; however, the time spent together during our Reserve weekend training was speedily eclipsed within the first few weeks in Iraq. What had been casual friendships rapidly grew into strong bonds that went far beyond—we were brothers-in-arms. While outside the wire, we spent every waking minute together. While not conducting operations, we would workout, eat, and otherwise pass the time together. Our team was composed of four combat engineers and our team's driver. Sergeant GG, commanded the team. From a rural area of Virginia, GG had a relaxed demeanor and a slow Southern drawl. The only one of our team with a wife and kids, he liked to crack a joke but always made sure we were prepared to do our jobs. He walked the line between friend and leader exceptionally well. Corporal Parrott, from Tennessee, wasn't part of Charlie Company prior to deployment. Rather, he was a member of a sister company based in Knoxville but had volunteered to deploy in order to help fill Charlie Company's ranks. He was smart, serious and had a singular focus on our mission. Above all, he wanted to see combat. He was probably the least social of the entire platoon. Seemingly always grumpy and, at times, outright hostile; it took weeks to warm to him. Once we did, and once he began to open up, we found that we had a fierce friend that liked to joke around and could be counted on in any situation.

Lance Corporal Sherman, the fourth engineer in our team, was from a small town in Virginia. He was the epitome of the nice, polite Southern gentleman. Of the group, he was perhaps the most laid back. When not conducting operations, he would read books on personal finance and attempted to teach himself German. Lance Corporal Hayne was the only one in our group that wasn't a combat engineer. He was from the same part of Virginia as Sherman, and the two had been close friends prior to the deployment. Towards the latter half of our deployment, he was separated from us and permanently stationed on Camp KV to work with the crew maintaining the vehicles.

It took a few weeks of conducting operations before we became fully integrated and accepted into the broader infantry and LAR teams. Over time, the benefits of combat engineers were generally recognized and the routine with one team conducting operations, while the other team remained in KV, coalesced into the norm. After several days "out in the field" or "outside the wire" conducting operations with the grunts and maintaining around-the-clock watch, we were usually exhausted and ready for a break. Then, after a few days back in Camp KV, we were ready to go back out. Most units in Iraq at the time didn't operate in this way. Instead, they would typically leave their bases for specific missions that generally lasted no more than a day or two. Although it may have been a less comfortable way to spend a deployment, especially in the winter months, by remaining out in the field for longer periods of time we were able to develop a better understanding of the terrain and area in which we were operating.

In this way, operations in our area became a systematic, routine process; with every Marine counting down the number of rotations outside the wire until we expected to return home. This process was occasionally punctuated by periods of increased activity such as the Iraqi elections and the Battle of Fallujah.

August 2004–October 2004: In-Country

USMC Base 29 Palms, CA—Kuwait—Al Asad, Iraq
August 12–August 26, 2004

I've got a lot to update from the last couple of weeks. After the week of leave, the last few days at 29 Palms were uneventful. We would have a short class or two each day and then be cut loose to "get our gear ready." At that point, there really wasn't much left to do, so we spent most of our time going to the gym, PX, movies, or just hanging out in the barracks. Dad bought me some clippers while I was on home leave, and I made an attempt to cut my own hair. I screwed it up so badly that I had to shave my head, which I'd half expected considering it was my first attempt. The only class that offered anything new was a talk given by Corporal Light. He's recently back from Iraq after having been wounded. He was in a city near the Syrian border and evidently saw a lot of action. It freaked out those of us in 2nd squad since we were already fairly certain, at that point, that we would be going to the same general area. His unit lost a lot of guys and his stories made Iraq sound like Vietnam, with ambushes being an everyday event. He talked about barely making it back to base from one ambush, only to be called out into the middle of yet another firefight. I'm obviously not in a position to criticize, but I got the sneaking suspicion that a lot of the stuff he was telling us was bullshit, or at least extremely exaggerated. If things were really as bad as he made it sound, then the daily casualty count would be much higher. That said, I suppose it could be true of a particular unit or city, with levels of violence cycling between different locations. But it's hard to believe that every city could have that level of sustained violence without casualties being significantly higher.

Other than those brief classes, I managed to kill most of my time with Miles, Meyers, Burdette and Weaver. A bunch of us went to see *Dodgeball*, which was OK. You could hear Strong's laugh from across the theatre. He's a Ben Stiller fan and can pull off a decent impression; he also has the loudest laugh I've ever heard. People around us were looking over, assuming that he was laughing super loud as a joke. Some of the guys drank in the evenings, but the majority of us were too worried about the possibility of a tough PT session the next morning. We did cut loose the last night prior to heading to the airport, which was a good time. The word was that we were to be bused to the airfield early the next morning, so we weren't allowed off base but could party in the barracks. It was a good night. GG and Weaver made a twenty dollar bet with me that I will chew tobacco or dip at some point during the deployment. While I don't expect to pick up chewing tobacco, I'll be surprised if I ever see the money. Later that night, since he hates Dave Matthews Band, GG went on the hunt for anyone that had a DMB CD. From across the barracks I heard him shout "Where's Davidson?" since he knew that I had one, but I was able to keep out of sight. In all, it was a fun way to spend our last night on U.S. soil. I wrote a rambling letter which I never intend to mail, and then went to sleep fairly early.

We woke up early on August 15th and, with a lot of the guys still a little drunk, loaded onto the buses for a final few stops prior to heading to the airfield. We ate chow, drew our weapons from the armory, and then loaded back onto the buses to head to March AFB. Once we got to the base and unloaded, we were put into a hangar by the tarmac and told to wait until the flight was ready. There were some USO volunteers who gave out care packages while we waited and we otherwise killed time by watching the U.S. basketball team lose to Puerto Rico in the Olympics. It seemed like a long wait, particularly because a lot of us had hangovers. After a while, we finally boarded the plane for the flight. We weren't the only unit on the flight and, as we were loading, there were people patrolling the line of Marines getting on the plane. For some reason they didn't want anyone taking photos of the flight line or the plane. I'm not sure why; it was just a normal commercial plane and didn't appear to contain any sensitive or classified units or cargo. Although, I've never heard the name of the airline before, so maybe they are trying to protect the flights loaded with troops that have layovers in other countries.

Sometime early in the morning of the sixteenth, we stopped to refuel in Bangor, Maine. That brief stop provided a sharp reminder of all the good times I'd had while visiting Maine last summer. Things have taken quite a turn since then. Once we took off again, it felt like we were finally leaving home—for the next seven or more months, we'll be half a world away. While I'm obviously going to miss family, one of my major regrets is that I'll miss out on graduating with my friends at school. I suppose some of my memories of the coming year may be more interesting from an outside perspective, but the fact is that I'd rather have the fun, if unremarkable, college memories rather than whatever is in store for me here.

I spent most of the flight watching movies and reading, but couldn't manage to get any sleep. The flight was punctuated with yet another stop along memory lane as we next touched down in Frankfurt, Germany. It's hard to believe that just a couple months ago I landed at the same exact airport, looking forward to a summer of traveling around Europe and studying in Berlin. Uncle Sam had different plans. We had a longer layover in Frankfurt, so I was able to shoot off a couple emails from the USO center. We eventually loaded back up to head to our final destination of Kuwait. It was interesting to fly over the Black Sea, then over Ankara, Turkey—I've never been so far east. The pilot made an announcement as we flew over Baghdad. It was eerie to look down on the city. Even though it is a city wracked by daily violence, it looked so peaceful from the sky. It was midnight by the time we landed finally in Kuwait. Looking out the window, I could see the lights from a fleet of ships in the Persian Gulf. I suppose they were oil tankers or other commercial ships. I could also see the flames from the oil pipes flickering on the ground as we flew over both Iraq and Kuwait. As we landed, Burdette started singing "This is the end ... my only friend, the end." It's good to have someone with a dry sense of humor around. Even at midnight, the TV screen in the plane said the outside temperature was over 100°.

We offloaded from the plane and were crammed straight onto buses, practically sitting on top of one another, while sweating in the night's heat. On the way to the base, I could see cars pulled off the side of the road in the desert with TVs on. We were later told that it's something that the Arabs do for fun. To cool off, they drive into the desert, set up TVs on the car's hood or in a popped open trunk, and sit around watching TV. We were bused to a base called Camp Victory, which is a huge tent city with a berm around it. It must be one of the main transit bases in Kuwait, as units seemed to be coming and going all the time, with seemingly no one permanently stationed there. After arriving, we set up a line to unload our gear out of the trucks that had followed us from the airport. By this time, the sun was coming up, so we took pictures of each of the squads, and then of the entire platoon. Upon inspection in full daylight, the base was actually a pretty nice place. It wasn't really too dissimilar from a base in the States, with the exception of the lack of permanent buildings. The chow hall had a good breakfast, and there were all kinds of fast food trailers scattered around. There were even little trailers, which housed shops selling everything from clothes to jewelry but they weren't open yet, so we never had a chance to check them out.

We weren't in Camp Victory very long before we were loaded back onto buses and taken to another airfield. We had originally flown into the Kuwaiti International Airport, but the next flight took off from what must have been a Kuwaiti military base. We waited in a warehouse or hanger for a few hours, until finally boarding a C-130 to fly to the largest Marine base within Iraq—Al Asad Airbase. While killing time in the hangar, I messed around with the GPS that Dad had given me but I couldn't get it to work properly. Despite the fact that the flight to Iraq was really uncomfortable, as we were half sitting on the webbing seats and half on our piles of gear—I slept almost the entire way. Nervous excitement can only keep you going for so long; I woke up briefly as we were circling for landing, only to fall back asleep again. I was still in a groggy daze when we were told to grab our gear and run out of the back of the C-130, which had landed while I was asleep. As I ran out, my first thought was "Holy shit, it's hot here!," and it took a minute to realize that the blast of heat I felt was from the backwash of the plane. After disembarking, we sat by the side of the airfield, sweating in the sun, until we were finally bused to Camp Dawghouse—a smaller camp within Al Asad. Al Asad is an absolutely massive former Iraqi airbase. We saw destroyed Iraqi planes every once in a while; Camp Dawghouse, a small tent city with a couple permanent buildings, is set alongside an old runway with a couple of huge bomb craters in it. After the long, two-day journey, we were all exhausted and crashed in a big tent that was set up for incoming units. I was lucky enough to snag a bunk next to the AC air duct pumping cold air into the tent, and I slept like a rock.

We've been in Al Asad for a while now, getting acclimated to our surroundings and going through some last minute checks and classes. We've spent more time practicing with the 14s (mine detectors), were given an overview of our AO (Area of Operations), a review of the types of UXO often found, and have had refresher classes on how to properly call for air support or a medical evacuation. We've also spent a few afternoons going through IED immediate action drills with vehicles, which may be the most useful training we've done since being called up. Prior to this, we've always done IED drills while on foot but, from the sound of it, we'll be in vehicles a good portion of our time outside the wire. For the drills, we load into vehicles and form a convoy, driving around until one of the SSgts calls over the radio, "IED, vehicle number so and so." Then we all jump out to form a perimeter and evacuate the "casualties." From what we've been hearing, this is the most probable type of action that we'll see in Iraq, which is disconcerting. It's not exactly the pitched battles that you picture in your mind's eye. Aside from classes, we've been given a decent amount of free time, which I've spent sleeping, reading, calling home from the phone center, watching movies in the platoon tent, or playing ping-pong at the MWR (Morale, Welfare, and Recreation) tent. The Dawghouse portion of Al Asad is a slightly more rustic version of Camp Victory, which itself was a more rustic version of a stateside base. All in all, it's pretty comfortable.

Although it feels like a stateside base, it didn't take long for the Iraqis to remind us that we are now in a place where the majority of the population would be happy to see us dead. On the third or fourth morning at Dawghouse, while we were at morning chow, we heard a loud boom. It wasn't a pop or bang like a rifle shot, but rather that really deep rumble that sounds like it's coming from the center of the earth. Everything in the chow hall vibrated and rattled. The chatter

51

immediately stopped, and we all silently listened. Then we heard an even louder boom. All fifty or sixty people in the chow hall had the same instinctive reaction to duck. In retrospect it was kind of funny; we all ducked down to take "cover" under the chow hall's flimsy plastic tables. By the third boom, we were all up and running back to our tents to put on flak jackets. As we ran, I could see the impacts hitting near a flight line across a stretch of desert from our camp, where a line of planes and helicopters were parked. The explosions were kicking up huge plumes of dirt, but were well off to the side of the planes. The Dawghouse portion of Al Asad is actually relatively close to the wire fence that surrounds the base and, even though I knew it wouldn't happen, I was hoping that there would be some kind of assault. At the time, we assumed the explosions were from mortars, but we found out later that it had actually been a rocket attack. The insurgents usually rig them to fire long after they're gone. There had been a total of seven or eight rockets and the impacts were pretty large, larger than most mortars. Up until then, at least in my mind, Al Asad had felt like a more rustic version of 29 Palms. Both are shitholes in the desert. But after the rocket attack, I think we all realized that we're in a war zone.

Thus far, we've only done one mission outside the wire with the entire platoon. We joined some of the 1st CEB engineers that we'll be replacing and went to Dulab, a huge former Iraqi ASP (Ammunition Supply Point) from Saddam's time. The place is just a massive section of desert, with square berms of dirt built up every so often—almost like little square forts. The Iraqi Army stored their ammo in the middle of the squares, out in the open, since everything is so dry it didn't need to be covered. To destroy the ASP during the invasion, we were told that the Army had dropped bombs on the squares, but that this only resulted in the ammo being scattered and damaged. Most of what we saw were mortar and artillery shells. Since it's too large of an area to guard completely, the insurgents sneak in at night to take as many shells as possible to use in making IEDs. I can't help but think that we must be short of manpower. The area should be cleared of all ammo immediately, and the place should be fully guarded until the last shell is destroyed. Every shell the insurgents are able to take will later be used to try and kill Americans. Instead, we put a platoon out each night to try and catch the insurgents, but it's such a large area that our presence really only serves as a minor nuisance.

We also set some booby-traps on a few of the shells. Not the kind that would blow up if anyone disturbs them, but ones that will pop a flare if someone tries to pick up the shell. Of course we don't want to be potentially hurt by our own booby-traps, so we had to clearly mark the shells with white paint. The result is that the insurgents rarely, if ever, end up touching them. They may not be able to read what is written on the shell, but they can certainly tell which ones look different from the others. We spent all day picking up shells and carrying them to a huge pile, where EOD eventually blew them up. It was tiring work, but the explosion made it worthwhile; it was the biggest I've ever seen. They make a daily announcement on Al Asad, which is miles away, prior to explosions like that, to warn that it's not an attack.

The only other mission that guys from our platoon have done since being in-country was a leaders' recon of the AO. They went down to FOB Hit, near the city of the same name, to get a feel for the area. As the convoy was leaving FOB Hit to head back to Al Asad, one of the vehicles ran over a landmine. The guys had to jump out and set up a perimeter until the seven-ton truck which hit the mine, could be fixed. One of our guys was in the vehicle that got hit but no one was hurt, it just blew off a tire. It really drives home the seriousness of the matter, I'm starting to believe this 15% casualty number. When you think about it, we haven't been here long or done much, but we've already seen a rocket attack and a mine strike. The odds are fairly likely that if things keep up at this pace, our platoon will suffer a casualty.

Camp Korean Village, Iraq
August 27, 2004

Today was the day that no one had been looking forward to—our squad has separated from the platoon. We're still holding out some hope that we will get back together at some point, but I seriously doubt it. In some ways, it's nice. There will be less oversight without the SSgts and Captain around, but we'll miss the rest of the guys. Besides, it's nice to have the support structure that comes with having some rank.

53

The highest ranking guy we'll have is Sergeant Wallace. It looks like the rest of the platoon won't be divvied out to the different infantry companies as we had expected, they'll be able to support them all from Al Asad. At least, that's the plan for the moment. Those lucky bastards not only get to stay together but also have a pretty decent base to live on. The only reason we have been separated is because Alpha Company is being sent too far away to be directly supported from Al Asad.

We found out a couple days ago that we would be going to FOB Korean Village, near the city of Ar Rutbah and the Syrian and Jordanian borders. Before leaving, we asked around to find out what we could. We wanted to know how often the base gets mortared or patrols are ambushed, and were able to briefly meet with one of the 1st CEB guys that had been stationed there. He said the base was pretty shitty compared to Al Asad, at least in regards to creature comforts. A rumor had recently circulated that an engineer was shot while setting up some wire around the FOB, but the 1st CEB guy hadn't heard anything about it. On top of that, he didn't seem too worried, so I doubt it happened. He told us that the city of Ar Rutbah isn't next to the FOB, so there's zero chance of any snipers near the base. I have no idea how stories like this get started; someone obviously must make them up out of thin air. We've also heard that about 80% of the hardcore insurgents are Syrian and that a lot of them cross over the border near FOB KV. He couldn't really comment on that and, in general, didn't really have much to tell us that we didn't already know. He talked about the type of food on base, the living quarters, and the types of missions that we'll be doing. It sounds like they largely avoided the city, focusing more on protecting the roadways, which, from a casualty perspective, is probably the safest course.

We said our goodbyes to the rest of the platoon and hopped on a shuttle to a different airfield. After sitting around for a while, we were loaded onto one of the big CH-53 helicopters for the flight to KV—my first helicopter ride. It was hot and smelled like diesel fumes. The helicopter felt like it was swerving from side to side. That motion, coupled with the smell of the German shepherd bomb-sniffing dog I sat next to, made me sick and I spent the entire flight trying not to throw up. When we got off the helicopter, it was like a scene from *Platoon*. We walked off the back with all of our gear, a little dazed as we took in our new surroundings. As we disembarked, a guy in a litter with an IV in his arm was being loaded onto a medical Black Hawk helicopter. We heard later that he'd been hit by an IED that afternoon. A pretty sobering greeting to KV.

Camp KV was at one time a small Iraqi town of about thirty small white houses, surrounded by a white wall. It sits off the side of the interstate called Route Mobile and is located about half way between the nearest Iraqi city of Ar Rutbah and the border crossings into Syria and Jordan. Most of the houses serve as the operations center, chow hall, medical center, and officers/senior NCO quarters. They've knocked holes in the white wall around the village in a couple places, so that those of us in the tent city just outside the wall can get in and out. The houses and tent city are surrounded by a large berm with guard towers set up every so often. One of the infantry squads will have to man the berm and towers, which will be an intensely boring job, as there doesn't seem to be anything around KV for miles in any direction. As an attachment squad to the grunts, I'm still anxious to see how they'll use us. I think some of the guys in our squad would be OK with being put on guard duty but I'm praying that we aren't.

We've been set up in one of the big tents in the tent city. There are about twenty of these tents, but less than half seem to be occupied. They aren't the typical green military tents, but rather are some kind of Arab nomad-looking tents; they're brown and have plywood floors on the inside. Each tent holds about fifty cheap, middle-eastern-made bunk beds. Much different conditions than what the rest of the platoon will be living in at Al Asad. Apparently, once the unit they are replacing finally heads home, they'll be moving into the little two-person "cans" which have power and air conditioning, much nicer than a tent shared with a few dozen people. The one saving grace is that there are a couple large AC units in each tent. The biggest downside, from what I can tell thus far, is the rats that live underneath the plywood flooring. With a tent full of guys eating and living, there are more than enough scraps for a little rat colony to thrive. At first glance, the facilities on KV don't seem bad. While on base, we'll be getting breakfast and dinner in the chow hall but we'll be issued MREs (Meals-Ready-to-Eat) for lunch. There aren't any showers, and the only bathrooms are some nearly overflowing porta-potties. Apparently the Iraqi contractor who empties them comes infrequently. One of the houses in the village is the phone and internet center, but evidently the connection is infrequent and slow. There is also a tent with a smattering of workout equipment, not much, but better than nothing. In general, I think things could be a lot worse.

So those are our digs, at least until we're moved somewhere new or are ordered to rejoin the platoon. Aside from a brief tour around the base, I haven't really had much of a chance to explore. All told, I can't complain. Guys in the invasion were sleeping on the ground and moving every day, while there's a good chance that we'll be staying in one place for the entire deployment. I'm sure that after a few weeks we'll have the tent set up more comfortably. There are enough bunks so that we don't have to share and some guys are already draping towels and sheets from the empty top bunk, to give some privacy to the bottom. The tents also have power, and Burdette has a portable DVD player, so we plan to set up a little lounge area. I'm anxious to get outside the wire and see what the AO is like. The changeover is supposed to happen relatively quickly, so I shouldn't have long to wait.

Camp Korean Village, Iraq
August 28, 2004

We spent the majority of the day sitting in one of the empty tents, suffering through briefing after briefing. Once most were finished, we waited for a Colonel to arrive. After waiting for forty-five minutes, the Colonel gave a typical, gung-ho Marine officer speech. The majority of it focused on the need to remain vigilant and not get complacent. He did capture our attention when he told a story about three Marine snipers in Ramadi that had fallen asleep in their observation post and were found shot in the head. My immediate question, though I remained silent, was "How do we know that they fell asleep"? At any rate, he followed that up with a couple other stories which seemed to be meant to shock. I'm guessing the reason he talked so blasé about these types of attacks on his own troops was to drive home the brutal and unsentimental nature of this war, as if we needed a reminder. He'd probably be better served by saving his speech for halfway through the deployment, when we'll no doubt be over confident. At the moment, we're all pretty keyed up and ready to go. He also told us that one of the metrics they use to measure success in the AO is how much it costs the insurgents to pay someone to place an IED, which I thought was an interesting approach. Apparently, the insurgents find it too dangerous to do themselves so they outsource it; the price has gone from ten dollars per IED to fifty—capitalism at work.

Camp Korean Village, Iraq
September 1, 2004

I went on my first real mission last night. It wasn't exactly a full-blown combat mission, but it offered my first glimpse of an Iraqi city. Also, aside from the rocket attack, it was my first exposure to traces of the insurgents. Our fire-team was called to join one of the infantry squads in an open area of desert not far from the city. We rolled out of base just as the sun was setting. In some ways, this place can be quite beautiful. With no trees or geographic features to obstruct the view, there are some amazing sunsets.

My first sight of the city was at dusk and, from less than a mile distant, it looked like something out of *Lawrence of Arabia*. The city is as remote as any I've ever seen, with desert for mile upon mile in any direction. The remoteness is perhaps more from the knowledge that there isn't another major city for at least a couple hundred miles, rather than just the landscape alone. The minarets of the mosques seemed to be the only tall structures—all other buildings are generally brown or white squat, square structures. From where we were sitting, with the exception of the green lights on the mosques, it's not hard to imagine that this is what cities in the Middle East looked like five hundred years ago. I'm sure once we actually get inside the city it'll be a different story. It's likely packed with cars, TVs, and every other modern convenience. But, from a distance, I couldn't see anything that looked glaringly modern. By the time we joined the infantry and started to unload our gear, we could hear the loudspeakers of the mosques begin the evening prayers. It was kind of creepy. From a distance it sounded more like moaning or howling. Since there seem to be dozens of

The sun setting over the vast desert that stretches from Ar Rutbah, Iraq, south to Saudi Arabia and west to Syria and Jordan.

mosques, the loudspeakers overlapped one another, which made it sound even more bizarre. I stood there for a second to take it all in. Less than a month ago, I had been visiting home, fishing in the muddy Chickahominy River, and now I was standing in a desert in the Middle East looking at the minarets of an Iraqi city.

The reason that we were called out was because a local source, named the Goat Man, had reported an insurgent weapons cache to one of our patrols earlier in the day. He had pointed out an area in the desert where they had buried the cache, so we broke out the mine detectors and started to sweep. It didn't take long until we hit a loud signal and started digging. The insurgents had buried AKs, artillery shells, mortars, RPGs, and belts of ammo. Some were wrapped in plastic, but most were just stacked on top of one another. Nothing was buried too deep and although we used the mine detectors, it was easy to see where the insurgents had recently disturbed the dirt. The desert floor is actually pretty firm, not sandy like I had expected. We dug for quite a while, late into the night. It seemed like a lot of equipment but I suppose it's all relative—this may have been only a minor weapons cache for all I know.

The Goat Man and some of his kids were milling about when we first started sweeping. I can't help but wonder about his motivation for telling us. Apparently, he was given some food, money, and toys for his kids, as well as a dress for his wife, in exchange for the information. In all, it's probably not a bad haul for what looked like an extremely poor family. The guy lives in a small house with no power, so I'd be surprised if he did it for idealistic political reasons. I'm sure he knew we would pay him, but it still doesn't seem worth the risk. Perhaps he just doesn't want the insurgents to dominate the city. I suppose there's a chance that these people are more sophisticated than I give them credit for but, if I had to guess, I'd say he just didn't want this stuff on his land. Notifying us was the easiest removal option. Still, he's putting himself and his family at some considerable risk. His shack is one of the only structures nearby and given the remoteness of the location, it's pretty obvious that we didn't stumble across this random spot on our own.

Camp Korean Village, Iraq
September 2, 2004

I was in the area around the city again today. We found some more stuff near the weapons cache from the other night, mostly mortar rounds. We were on the way to visit the Goat Man and someone noticed a different section of disturbed earth that we'd missed the other night. We brought Goat Man some food and water while the HET (Human Exploitation Team) guy and a couple of the infantry grunts talked to him. We parked in a wadi to keep the vehicles out of sight, and killed time by playing with his kids. The rest of the day was spent setting up OPs along the roads near the city and doing MSR (Main Supply Route) security. Essentially, it was a tour of the area with the guys we are replacing, specifically the OPs that they regularly use along Routes Phoenix, Mobile, and Michigan.

I'm anxious to actually get into the city but it sounds like the guys we're replacing spent most of their deployment just outside of it, watching

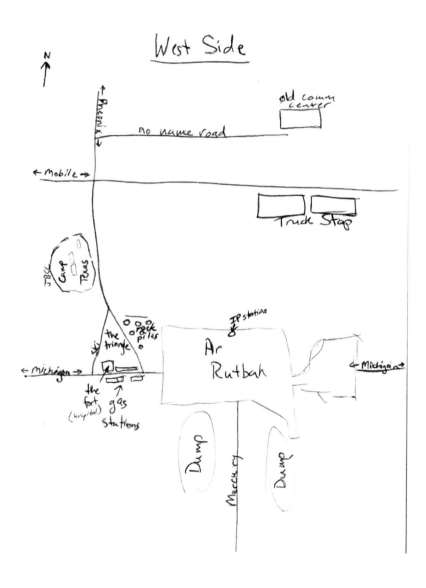

West Side

N

old comm center

no name road

← mobile →

Truck Stop

phoenix

JBCC Camp Texas

the triangle

rock piles

IP station

Ar Rutbah

← Michigan →

← Michigan →

the fort (hospital)

gas stations

Dump

Mercury

Dump

A sketch from the journal of the west side of the city of Ar Rutbah.

60

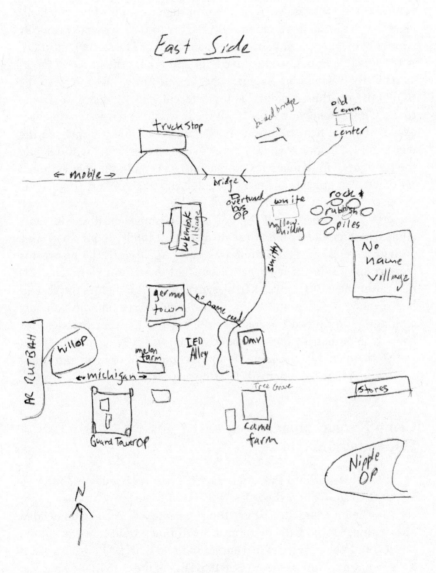

A sketch from the journal of the east side of the city of Ar Rutbah.

the roads. Today was split between sitting at OPs and going on two-vehicle roving patrols. We wandered through a couple of the small villages that are located around the city, but the routine seems to primarily consist of driving up and down the roads followed by setting up an OP. After a couple hours, we load back up and repeat the process. Occasionally, we'll also set up a vehicle checkpoint. We've all been given the BOLO (Be-on-the-Lookout) list for different vehicles that we're trying to snag. It was a hot and long day. It really wouldn't have been that bad, except that the heat is absolutely brutal. About midway through the day, it got to the point where I didn't even feel like drinking water, and the thought of food made my stomach turn; even in the shade, there's no relief. The only escape is by volunteering to go on a roving patrol. On patrol, you can sit in the back of the high-back Humvee and catch the breeze. We heard an IED go off in the distance on Route Phoenix while we were pulled off on the side of Route Mobile, about a half-mile away. It turned out that no one was hurt. Apparently, the insurgents were trying to hit a roving patrol but had their timing off. The IED blew after the first Humvee had already gone by but before the second had reached it. It felt a little strange to have no specific mission, just zipping up and down the roads to make sure that they are clear for convoys. Not that any mission is necessarily worth dying for but, if that were to happen, I would hope it would be on a raid or in an ambush—something where we're actually fighting rather than just driving around.

Camp Korean Village, Iraq
September 5, 2004

I finally went into the city today. We had received some intel on a couple of houses on the western edge of town, so we raided them early in the morning, just before the sun came up. The grunts needed one engineer to go with the breach team that would be entering the houses, so I volunteered. We went on the raid with LAR, driving from KV down Route Mobile. As we exited the interstate onto Route Phoenix, the drivers hit the gas and we came flying into the western side of the city—arriving just before dawn. Everyone was amped up since it was our first raid into the city, but it ended up being somewhat anticlimactic. We all jumped out of the vehicles and the assault teams rushed into the houses, but there was no resistance. There was some confusion as we got out of the vehicles and the grunt squad I had joined as part of the breach team ended up being part of the cordon around the target houses, so I spent my time standing guard in an alley. We were all alert and ready-to-go for the first fifteen minutes, but after that the adrenaline faded and the mood became less tense. By the time the assault teams were finished searching the houses, the sun had come up and it didn't feel tense at all. I could smell fresh bread being baked as the city came to life and the noise of morning traffic began to pick up; it was actually kind of pleasant. Apparently, we didn't get the guy we were looking for, but we did find an RPK machinegun in his house. As we were leaving the city, women were waving and kids were giving us the thumbs-up.

I suppose this is how insurgencies are fought: getting the weapons off the streets and keeping the bad guys on the run, not a stand-up-and-fight slugfest like you see in the movies. It was an odd experience.

A Light Armored Vehicle (LAV) operated by the 3rd Light Armored Reconnaissance (LAR), in position during a raid in the city of Ar Rutbah.

I had pictures in my head of a dilapidated, third world mess-of-a-city. Instead, it seemed like a relatively normal, modern place. Of course it's different than a U.S. city, but not vastly so. If anything, it almost felt somewhat European. As people were getting up and heading out to work, it didn't seem like a war zone at all, so much so that I felt like a bit of a jackass for standing around with a rifle. We had been so pumped about the raid, it later almost felt ridiculous as people were passing us, waving as they went on their way to work. We were ready for *Black Hawk Down* and it ended up being nothing even remotely close. I guess that's why people get complacent. It may be quiet like this for the next twenty raids and then, on the twenty-first, it could all blow up, and the whole city may turn out to attack us. The fact that we found a machine gun in the guy's house is a testament to that.

Camp Korean Village, Iraq
September 7, 2004

My parents forwarded an email to me that had been circulating around the Charlie Company network of parents and wives. It was entitled MORNING NEWS and was written in all caps, like an urgent telegram. Apparently, someone back home had seen something on the news about seven Marines being killed in Iraq. The email sounded panicky about the possibility that the causalities could be guys from Charlie Company, and it discussed how people would be notified ASAP of any updates or news. It serves as a reminder of just how hard this will be for the families back home. There are thousands of Marines in Iraq, and there's a good chance that some will die almost every day of our deployment. Every little news blimp or mention of casualties is going to weigh heavily on their minds, even though it is a reasonably slim probability that it will be someone from our company.

It's almost easier being the one over here, we only have ourselves to worry about. There's no need to lie in bed, wondering if your loved one is still alive. As much as it may suck to be here, at least in that regard there's no ambiguity or unknowns. We go on missions and hopefully aren't killed or injured. Pretty simple, really. There's no point wondering if you'll be hit, and I don't think casualties are high enough to really prompt too many concerns. Or, if anyone does think much about it, they certainly don't stress about it. This isn't World War I or Vietnam. I saw a news clip stating that casualties for 2004 were at the pace of one to two killed per day which, with something like 100,000+ troops in Iraq, is less than 1%. That said, the total number of combat troops may be significantly less, maybe 1/3rd of the total, but it's still a low probability. For the families at home, that's no consolation. They have no idea what we are doing or where we might be at any given time. When Dad is in a meeting at work, he has no idea whether his only son is in the middle of a fire fight, already dead, or just asleep in his rack. It really must be hell for them and I can't help but feel sorry that I'm putting them through this. I have to be mindful to email often to make this as easy as possible. I have already decided that, no matter what happens, I'll tell them that it's boring and that we don't leave the base much. They'll probably assume that I'm just trying to comfort them, but it can't hurt.

Camp Korean Village, Iraq
September 9, 2004

Now that we've been here a while, things have started to fall into a bit of a routine. We tend to go outside the wire in twelve-hour shifts, with the occasional raid mixed in. I went out again yesterday. Most of the time was spent on watch at various OPs, or driving around on two-vehicle roving patrols. We've been going out with the infantry during the day, while the LAR units goes out at night. The LAVs they drive have much better night-vision equipment than our goggles or scopes. At first, I was happy not to have the night shift but, although it may mess with sleep, it might be worth it. The heat while on watch during the day is absolutely miserable. There's no escape when you're on watch and sitting in the turret of the Humvee, or up on a high point nearby. But even while not on watch, everyone huddles around the shade of the vehicles, and it's still cooking. Heat aside, it also seems like the flies disappear at night. I'm not sure how cool it'll get here in the winter, but I doubt it'll actually get cold.

At one point, when we were set up on an OP near the city, we heard

A hardback Humvee keeping watch from the south side of Ar Rutbah.

popping that almost sounded like gunshots. Without anyone saying a word, we all stopped chatting and listened. It continued at sporadic intervals but stopped after a while. While it may seem strange to us, every family in this country supposedly owns an AK-47, like every family owns a car back home. The shots, if that's what they were, could have been a wedding celebration for all we know. Still, it got me thinking that if the city wanted to take us on, there's very little that a few hundred Marines could do to stop a city of thousands.

Camp Korean Village, Iraq
September 11, 2004

We went on a massive raid yesterday to the west of KV, near the borders, targeting a big truck stop. We were told that the insurgents have been using it as a transit point where the foreign fighters supposedly get dropped off at the truck stop, then wait until someone picks them up to take them deeper into Iraq. We didn't know about the raid in advance. Sergeant Wallace woke me up in the middle of the night to let me know that Quinn and I had been picked to go. He said that the grunts were expecting contact and that he had already put together all the demo charges I may need for breaching. I slept restlessly for a couple hours, but I was pumped to finally be going on what sounded like an aggressive mission with the potential to see action. After all, this is what we've been training for.

We loaded up early in the morning. It was probably as large a force as we can muster from all the units on KV, while still maintaining security on the borders and along Route Mobile. There were about a dozen LAVs and around fifteen Humvees and seven-ton trucks full of Marines. Our progress down Route Mobile was covered by a flight of Cobra helicopters. It was an impressive sight as we barreled down the road. The column of LAVs drove to the north of us, out in the desert on what must have been a dirt road, since they have better off-road capabilities. The Humvees and seven-tons stuck to the highway. The helos were split between covering our column and covering the LAVs. With such a show of force, it's easy to see why the insurgents stick to hit-and-run tactics. With just AKs and mortars, anyone with the intention of getting in a standup fight with us would be killed before they could get a shot off.

In the end, the raid was a bust. Either the insurgents knew we were coming, or the intel wasn't good to begin with, because we didn't find shit. For all I know, the intel may have been that they only occasionally use the truck stop, but nothing regarding particular days or times. Even if it's used frequently, it's likely empty more often than it's full, so raiding it would be a shot in the dark anyway. I just assumed that they had some specifics, given how we were rolling out in force. At any rate, we rushed in like madmen on a bunch of bewildered truck drivers, but it didn't take long for things to calm down after we realized nothing was there. I spent most of my time helping to search some of the trucks in the parking lot. Some of the truck drivers were clearly freaked out. They came from Jordan or Syria, where life is chugging along like normal and just after crossing the border, they're suddenly in a war zone with a bunch of Marines pointing rifles at them and screaming in a language they don't understand. It would be nice to get a full briefing prior to a raid like you see in the movies, where everyone sits around looking at maps and pictures of particular targets. If we had an understanding of why we were raiding the truck stop, what our odds of finding something may be, or where the intel came from, then we would feel much more engaged. Or, at least, I would. It's mentally exhausting to prep for these missions and get yourself psyched up while operating in a vacuum of information.

Camp Korean Village, Iraq
September 14, 2004

More MSR security, OPs, and vehicle patrols. We have been going into the villages that lie outside the city more frequently. Nevertheless, sitting in the back of a Humvee staring at the side of the road for signs of an IED gets tedious after a few hours, let alone a few days. Apparently, the new plan is for us to start doing more frequent patrols into the city itself, with the intention of ensuring that the focus of the insurgents is on us, rather than on planting IEDs on Route Mobile. The insurgents used to IED Route Mobile fairly frequently but we haven't seen any since taking over the AO. The guys we replaced would spray paint a mark on the side of the road where an IED had either been found or gone off. When we first started, the ING (Iraqi National Guard) had a VCP (Vehicle Check Point) set up on Mobile near the off-ramp on to Route Phoenix and there were a cluster of these marks right in front of the VCP, so it's probably a good thing that they aren't around anymore.

I'm OK with doing more in the city; it keeps things much more interesting. I've done a couple patrols and raids thus far, and prefer going on foot rather than riding in the Humvees. It feels a little safer—sitting in a Humvee presents too large of a target and the feeling that you can't freely maneuver. From the little bit that I've seen of Ar Rutbah, it's a pretty foul city, though not as bad as I had expected. Parts look nice and who knows, maybe it's great by Iraqi standards. But the whole place smells like diesel fuel from all the leaky gas stations, and dog piss from the hordes of stray dogs. There's also an ever-present mass of kids all over the place. I'm guessing that school isn't a high priority in this part of the world. We heard that the estimated population of the city is anywhere from 30,000 to 50,000. I'm not surprised that they can't pinpoint the number. Even though it's a relatively small area of land, each house seems to have a ton of people in it. It's like a clown car. When we pass by on patrol, they just come pouring out, one after the other, to watch. The kids crowd around us like dogs asking for treats, saying "mista, mista," and pointing to their mouths. The little girls are cute, because they usually just wave and look shy. It feels a little ridiculous to patrol with a pack of ten kids pestering you. The plus side is that it can be a good indicator. When we patrol in the same area and the kids *won't* come out of the house, then it's time to be on guard. During a patrol through the small village of Germantown, some of the kids were pointing at our Humvee and laughing. It was hit by an IED before we were in-country, and the metal around the back wheel is shredded. My first thought when we got the vehicle was that it made us look battle hardened, but I guess it gives the opposite impression.

The kids are smarter than one would think. The other day, a boy

A typical patrol through the city—taking cover while surrounded by local children. When the children wouldn't come outdoors, Marines knew to be alert.

lied to us, saying that he saw masked men put an IED on a bridge on Route Mobile—northeast of the village we call Lukenbok. We gave him candy and snacks for the info, thinking that it was only right to reward him. We called in the news and a roving patrol went down to the bridge to take a look, but nothing was there—little punk. I think we were all surprised to see a little kid lie so seamlessly to a group of armed, foreign strangers. I suppose his "normal" is quite a bit different from that of the average kid in the States. His story seemed plausible. In fact, it would be the perfect place to put an IED, as you could hit a convoy and possibly damage the bridge at the same time. If we couldn't use Mobile anymore, the only alternative would be to send our supply convoys down Route Michigan, directly through the city, which would be a terrible alternate route. In terms of logistics, the insurgents can look down on the bridge from Germantown, set off an IED, and race back to Ar Rutbah without much risk to themselves. I don't think we keep an around-the-clock watch on the bridge. In reality, it would be impossible to watch every bridge along the entire stretch of road in our AO without needing a lot more Marines.

On a positive note, the weather seems to be starting to cool off, if only a little. The first week we got here, Sherman's little thermometer was maxed out at 110° by 0900. But the other day, I was actually somewhat cold when riding in the back of the Humvee towards the city. Good to see that it's just like home—no pleasant transition between seasons, just brutally hot to really cold. The higher-ups recently announced a change to rotations out in the field that calls for three days off, three days on. I'm not sure how I feel about that yet, we have been doing twelve-hour rotations. The reasoning behind the shift is that it takes so long to load all the gear and do all the checks and logistical stuff necessary to go outside. It's too much of a pain in the ass for such short durations. They plan to create two different teams—each will have a mix of infantry, LAR, and our engineer squad. Because of this, it looks like we won't be seeing much of our other fire-team. While we're out, they'll be back at base and vice versa. Whichever team is on base will then be responsible for doing the helo patrols and conducting any raids that require much prep time.

The only problem with the new schedule is that it can be really boring sitting around KV for three straight days. There is a small tent

Myself (left) and Parrott (right) while on a helicopter patrol.

with some mismatched weights, so we workout every day that we're back on base. But other than that, we go to chow and sit around the tent watching DVDs. No matter how you cut it, days on base are long and boring. The bright side is that it forces me to read and write a lot. I've been consuming about one book every three days on my days off on KV. One of the other highlights of being on base is that I'm able to check email and get letters and packages. The rumor circulating is that the mail truck was recently hit by an IED, because we didn't get any for quite a while. When it finally did arrive, half of the mail was burnt and looked like it had been wet.

I'd like to see some real action sometime, but I don't know how promising that looks. Aside from the base being mortared occasionally or roving patrols getting hit by IEDs, our command hasn't seen much of the enemy. Besides, mortars and IEDs aren't exactly the kind of action I'm looking for. The other day, we were setting up an OP near the intersection of Routes Mobile and Phoenix, when we heard a large explosion about four hundred yards south on Phoenix. When we got there, we saw an Iraqi guy who had been blown apart while putting in an IED. There wasn't anything we could do at that point, some guys took pictures. It was interesting to come face-to-face with the enemy, or what was left of one, although it's just as likely that he wasn't actually an insurgent—rather just a guy trying to make a buck by putting in an IED.

Camp Korean Village, Iraq
September 17, 2004

Another day off. Nothing new, other than that I may have to go on a helo patrol later today. While practicing deploying in and out of the helicopters on the landing pad, I slammed my head against the top of the hatch while running down the ramp. Helos aren't exactly made for guys my height. It completely laid me out, everyone had to run around me. It felt like I'd been hit with a baseball bat. Luckily my helmet took the brunt of it, but that was one of the more embarrassing things I've done in a while.

Other than going to the computer center to write some emails and hitting up the gym-tent, there isn't much to do. The computers are so slow that in my allotted half hour I was barely able to login to my email. I read a forwarded email that stated that the UN declared our involvement in Iraq to be illegal. Oh well, short of Germany invading Poland again, I have a hard time seeing the international community coming together to sanction any conflict. It would take a serious act of one-sided aggression, although it looks like they might be right on this one. It's pretty clear that our reasons for going to war weren't based on hard evidence. On a happy note, I found a pile of books in the corner of the chow hall that people in the States had donated. I was getting dangerously close to running out of new material and have started reading *Beau Geste*, which seems somewhat appropriate given where I am.

Outside Ar Rutbah, Iraq
September 19, 2004

I went outside the wire yesterday and thought I'd bring my journal along to kill some time while not on watch. We've patrolled around the area and sat at an OP watching Route Mobile. There is a noticeably large influx of people coming into the city, or at least a greater amount of activity. There seems to be more and more traffic on the highway. We're not sure what the reason could be, but we've been told to keep a lookout and stay alert. I'm not sure of the exact dates, but I suppose it could have something to do with the Hajj.

Camp Korean Village, Iraq
September 24, 2004

We heard today that we may be heading to one of the posts on the border crossings. There are only two options: either Walid, on the Syrian border, or Trebil, on the Jordanian. The units on KV have been taking turns maintaining a small contingent at each border crossing. The grunts have been given the task of guard duty for KV, so it's likely going to be either a contingent from LAR or some of the artillery guys. We were told that any rotation to the borders would likely last for a few weeks, after which we would rotate back to KV for a couple weeks. I'm not sure how I feel about that prospect. From what I've heard, the border crossings are really exposed, small bases which sit right next to the highway. You don't have to worry about anyone shooting at you from across the borders but, in reality, you wouldn't have to worry about the Iraq side either. The border crossings have only a few outlying buildings, so any kind of attack would be an all-or-nothing proposition for the insurgents. Either the Muj would try to overrun the border posts or they wouldn't bother; there couldn't be any small-time ambushes since there's nowhere for them to run to afterwards. You also wouldn't have to worry too much about IEDs, since the guys on the borders don't do much patrolling. All day, every day is spent inspecting vehicles coming into the country. My only major concern would be that, if your job is to inspect cars, then a VBIED (Vehicle-Borne Improvised Explosive Device) could be driven right up to your position. The insurgents wouldn't even have to worry about figuring out a way to get the car bomb close to you. They could simply load up a car with shells and then get in line to be inspected. Anyone out there would be pretty exposed if the Muj wanted to try something like that.

There are also rumors circulating that we may be moved in the early part of November. Most rumors don't have any truth to them, so I'll believe it when we actually get the word to pack our bags. The only reason for a move in November would be to support the planned assault on Fallujah. But, with our AO encompassing the city of Ar Rutbah, the town of Akashat, the two border crossings, an important MSR, and a handful of villages—I think we've got a lot to handle. Particularly when considering that we are covering this much ground with just one infantry company and one LAR company: maybe three to four hundred total combat arms Marines. If they were to relocate either company, then the higher-ups would have to scramble to find replacements— which sort of defeats the purpose. We were also told that they want to cut down on the number of raids into the city, which is something of an about face from what we had been told only a few days ago. We've recently begun *increasing* our patrols and raids into the city. That said, I can understand the reasoning. The city doesn't really have any strategic significance other than the fact that a secondary supply route runs through it, so we're putting people at risk for no real purpose or objective. The main supply route, Mobile, runs well to the north of the city, and we're able to keep it secure. There's no real reason to piss off the natives if we don't have to. Besides, half of the time we seem to end up raiding the wrong building. We'll rush into some poor bastard's house only to hear one of the officers say something along the line of "I think we're in the wrong place," while they look at the map and talk on the radio.

I think the catalyst for this latest change in strategy was the recent actions of one of the infantry officers. Everyone's been talking about it. In his speeches to us, it's easy to tell that he's itching for a fight, which is fair enough, although it could just be the standard Marine officer gung-ho charade to try and fire up the men. In any case, the story is that one of the OPs was fired on from the edge of the city last week; nothing big; just some pot shots from a distance. Apparently he rolled up in a roving patrol about twenty minutes after it happened and, instead of having a gunner in the turret, he was sitting there himself, manning the weapon. After rolling up, he fired off twenty rounds in the direction of where they thought the initial shots had come from, even though everyone was shouting for him to stop. The latest I heard from GG was that he was almost relieved of command. The higher-ups don't want this place to explode like Ramadi or Fallujah, which they keep telling us it has the potential to do, just because one guy acted like a dumbass. In any case, there's no reason to stir the pot.

I've been feeling a little sick lately, with a bit of a sore throat. The tent is real dusty with that powdery "moon dust" that all the vehicles kick up, which probably doesn't help things. The moon dust has the consistency of talcum powder and gets on everything. That, combined with not really getting much sleep when we're outside the wire, is the likely cause. Lately I've been doing the first watch of the night when we're outside the wire, which is nice because I then get to sleep uninterrupted through the rest of night. The worst is when I draw watch either in the middle of the night, the second hour, or the second-to-last hour. If I get the second hour, then I'll try to sleep for the first hour before my shift, but it's not restful since I know that I'll be getting up soon. Then, after the hour of watch, there are only a couple more hours of sleep before everyone is up for the day. In the end you get a combined total of two hours of sleep, none of which is very restful. As miserable as sleeping in the field may be, it makes the first night back on KV feel like paradise. Sleeping in a bed in a temperature controlled tent, after being completely exhausted, is the best feeling. I usually crash for eight straight hours, if not more.

Camp Korean Village, Iraq
September 26, 2004

We're back on base today after going out for a twelve-hour shift yesterday. Apparently they haven't decided on a permanent transition to the three-day rotations yet. The word has, of course, changed. Now the rumors are that we *won't* be sent to the borders; instead, we may be heading back to Al Asad to join with the rest of our platoon—which would be awesome. I haven't had a proper shower since we left Al Asad almost a month ago and baby wipes don't really cut it. Some of the guys have built a makeshift shower, which is just a plywood stall with a water barrel on top and a drawstring. It's crude, but better than nothing. Creature comforts aside, the best part would be joining back up with the rest of our guys. It would be good to see Weaver, Meyers, and Miles again. It also wouldn't be bad to have the SSgts and Captain to look out for us, though I'm less concerned about that now than when we first split off. Initially I was afraid that the grunts would use us for the worst jobs that they didn't want to do themselves but, so far at least, they've been using us as we were meant—combat engineer support for their operations. Nothing more, nothing less. So I'd say we've built a good working relationship.

As much as we were initially concerned or may still grumble, Sergeant Wallace has done a good job at making sure that we're included and involved—which is harder than it sounds. It's not easy for a sergeant to stand up to a captain or major. After our initial reception at KV, when it felt like no one had been expecting us, I think we were all a little nervous. Hell, we could have probably gotten away with just hiding out in one of the tents furthest from the base and gone the entire deployment without anyone knowing we were there. It's somewhat reminiscent of that Hackworth book, where he talks about people moving from unit to unit whenever they wanted in the Korean War. There may be all kinds of bureaucracy and computer systems at home, tracking everyone and every piece of equipment, but out in the field things are still pretty fluid. If no one was looking for you, an individual could just float along.

Camp Korean Village, Iraq
September 28, 2004

I still don't know if, or when, we are moving. We've been here for over a month so if they are planning on moving us then I hope it happens soon. There's no point in getting to know an AO, only to be moved with only a few months left in the deployment. While it would be nice to get back to our platoon, I'm getting pretty comfortable with where we are; both from an operational standpoint and the living conditions at KV. In its own way, this is actually a pretty beautiful spot. I jumped in the back of one of the seven-ton trucks that was parked by the perimeter berm the other night and watched the sunset. If there's one nice thing about this place, it's that it gives you time to think. I would never sit down to watch the sunset at home, even if I had the time. After the sun had gone, I laid down on the bench and watched as the stars came out. With such good visibility, the sheer number of stars in the sky makes it feel like the night isn't dark at all. I couldn't count to twenty seconds without seeing a shooting star. Either I hadn't noticed before, or there was a particularly large amount last night. In any case, it was a calming thing to do. People would probably be better served by doing that once a month, rather than paying to go to a shrink. It had a way of putting my mind at ease and calming my spirit.

The other night we set up an OP near the east side of the city and stayed there all night. The mosques started playing music at a weird hour, then the music stopped and there was some kind of announcement. The translators later said the Imam was telling the people to stay away from the Americans, especially while driving, and to expect attacks in the next few days. Apparently we caught some big guy in a recent raid and they are pissed about it. It's probably all for show. I doubt that they'll really attack us, but it's good PR for them. I had a two-hour watch from 0300 to 0500 and was really dragging by the end. For some reason the mosque loudspeakers were going almost the entire time, which was unusual. I don't know if it was just because I was really tired, but after a while the voices from the mosque started to sound like strange violin music. Maybe it was just the way the sound carried in the air, but it was soothing and nearly put me to sleep. At one point, it struck me just where I was. All of my friends are back at school, the only concerns are where the next party will be and the occasional class or test. Meanwhile, in the middle of the night, I'm sitting next to an old, blown up Iraqi AA (Anti-Aircraft) battery on a hill outside of some city in the Middle East, listening to prayers from a mosque. Sometimes it still doesn't feel real.

Camp Korean Village, Iraq
September 30, 2004

We went outside the wire for about eighteen hours yesterday. We started off the day with a raid in the morning, then patrolled and set up OPs for the rest of the time. We actually targeted a few different houses in the raid. Although I'm still not 100% sure whether it was intentional, or whether we just accidentally hit the wrong house on the first couple tries. I'm guessing it was the latter. Things started to have an air of ridiculousness as we would race up, jump out of the vehicles, smash open the door with the sledgehammer, and then rushed into each room like a SWAT team—only to be told by the interpreter and Captain that we should do it all over again a couple houses down the road.

I can't help but feel like an asshole by bursting into someone's house in the middle of the night, blindfolding them, zip tying their hands, and carting them off in front of their wife and kids—even if they may be potential bad guys. I guess the problem is that nobody that we take ever looks like they could be bad. It's not like a movie, where the villain looks like a villain. They always just look terrified and, in yesterday's case, fairly young. We took four yesterday and were told that two were on some kind of list, so I guess I shouldn't let my friendly inclination fool me. While I'm feeling sorry for them, they would probably be more than happy to saw my head off. They didn't have any weapons that we could find, which in itself is somewhat suspicious considering every house seems to have several. I was told by the HET guy that we took them because their stories didn't line up. Some said they weren't family but were meeting at the house in order to go to an early Morning Prayer session. Others didn't mention anything about the prayer session, but said that they were family visiting from out of town. While that's not necessarily proof of wrongdoing, this isn't exactly a place where suspects are given Miranda Rights. If we think there is cause for suspicion, then you're getting detained. Pretty simple. We let the interrogators or whomever deals with them next decide whether to release them.

After we blindfolded the four guys, we drove in circles in the desert for about an hour before finally taking them to KV. I guess the intention was to confuse and disorient them but, if they are actual insurgents, then they likely know that KV is the only U.S. base nearby. I'm starting to understand why the vast majority of people scowl at us. We're not exactly winning the hearts and minds with all these raids. Unless there's really good evidence, we would probably be better served by just leaving these people alone. To the normal Iraqis, with all the raids and road blocks and random searches, we're probably more of a hassle than any-

Blindfolded detainees from a raid in Ar Rutbah being held outside the city, awaiting transfer to Camp Korean Village.

thing else. And while it might be worthwhile to them if we were providing a significant degree of security, at least in our AO, I'm not sure that we do. We don't, nor can we, make things run smoothly in the city. It's a corrupt mess, just like it was when we didn't have many troops in the area. But it's also likely how it was under Saddam. Really, we can only provide security when we're actually there—in the city. But that doesn't last long, and the regular people have to live among the insurgents after we're gone. We'd probably be best off by just keeping the MSR open and clear of IEDs so our supply convoys can safely get through, only raiding the city when we have real solid intel.

Having gotten feedback on some of the interrogations, both during raids and those conducted back in base, there seems to be a huge, and somewhat bizarre, cultural difference. This shouldn't come as a surprise except that it's not the kind of cultural difference that I would have expected. In the U.S., being caught in a lie might be embarrassing, but over here people lie about the simplest of things, even if it's something that definitely doesn't need to be lied about. I thought truthfulness was a universally accepted positive trait, but it's been almost impossible to get the truth out of people when we question them. I could understand if it were simply a matter of us being Americans, and therefore they're naturally tight lipped. If nothing else, they would do so for the safety of their families, as the insurgents likely pay people a visit if they noticed that we stopped by. But these people tend to lie about the simplest things, and the lies are sometimes so fantastical that you can't believe that they'd think it could be plausible. It's easy to forget that they live in a weird blend of the modern and medieval ages. The other day while at an OP I saw a guy pull over to the side of the road and get out of his car. I thought he might be planting an IED so I watched him, but he quickly squatted down and took a shit, wiping his ass with his hand and only cleaning it with a little water after. The same day, Thomas the translator started arguing with an Iraqi that we were questioning. We asked Thomas what was going on, and he said that the Iraqi was claiming that the Americans were driven out of Fallujah last April because Allah dropped spiders on them from the sky. The guy was so emphatic about it that there was no doubt that he absolutely believed what he was saying. In fact, it seemed like he was gloating to us about it. So on one side, you have people that believe in fairy tales while, on the other, every hovel in every village seems to have a satellite dish on the roof. On top of that, there are a surprising number of decent-looking Mercedes driving around. Such a bizarre place. I would have to live here a long time before I could get to the point where I understood their world view; it's like talking to aliens.

Outside Ar Rutbah, Iraq
October 3, 2004

I've been going out a lot lately and expect it will continue for the foreseeable future. Apparently the idea of sticking to three or four day rotations has been put on hold. I can't complain, time out in the field seems to move at twice as fast as sitting around KV. Although it is nice to have a break to decompress. Outside the wire, every movement I make is on the orders of someone else. After a sustained amount of time, it gets incredibly frustrating. It's nice to be able to eat when you're hungry, rather than when someone tells you to quickly eat chow because you're going on a roving patrol in ten minutes.

Yesterday I blew up some UXO on my own for the first time. It was just a couple of tank rounds that were found in a tunnel in the old Iraqi military complex on the east side of the city. It's a good OP that we've used a few times, primarily because the complex has guard towers at each corner; hence the name "Guard Tower OP" that we've been using. We were double-checking the area for UXO when we came across the shells. It was a hell of a lot more fun to set up the explosives on my own, without all of the safety steps and checks required in training. In training there is always someone looking over your shoulder. Also in training, I've only ever done just one step in the process. This is the first time that I've done a shot from start to finish and fortunately, I didn't blow myself or anyone else up. It was actually pretty straightforward. I cut a half stick of C4, tied it with det cord, and set the timing fuse to a blasting cap. Although it was overkill, I had the grunts stop traffic on Route Michigan until the charge went off. Since the tank shells were in a tunnel there was almost no chance of pieces flying around, but I figured I'd rather be safe than sorry. The grunts seem to be using us more often now, which is nice. I think they're starting to trust us and realize that we're not complete idiots. That, and there are some things that we can do for them which actually makes their lives easier, or at least somewhat safer. While tank shells can't really be used as IEDs because they're directional, the more UXO we clean up the better. At the very least, the material for making an IED won't be lying all over the place—which is a good first step.

The second half of the day I spent driving the Humvee. It was fun since I've never driven one before and it definitely made patrolling much less tedious than just riding in the back. But the drive back to KV that night was terrifying. It was myself with Quinn and one of the grunts. Things had been quiet on the radio all day. No IEDs or any other hijinks that we heard of. Despite this, for some reason it took a long time for all the squads to get to the rally point in order to make our way back to KV. By the time we were rallied up and ready to go, it was already dusk. I wasn't the original driver of the Humvee, so I didn't have any NVGs (Night Vision Goggles) and was starting to get worried about driving in the dark without them. I had the grunt run around to the other vehicles to ask, but no one had an extra set. Instead, we were told to follow a little closer than normal so that we could more easily make out the vehicle in front of us. We were also told that it shouldn't be a big deal as we would be getting back to KV well before it got really dark out.

I can't believe we didn't drive off the road on the way back. I've never concentrated so hard while driving. All three of us had our eyes glued to the road. Quinn was looking on the right side, while the grunt was watching the left. I concentrated straight ahead. By the time we were getting close to KV it was pitch black. I had finally reached the point where I decided to just turn on the lights. The way I saw it, there could be two outcomes. I'd either be told that I did the most sensible and safest thing, or I'd get chewed out for breaking protocol and putting the entire convoy at risk. While it would have likely been the latter, I figured that it was better than killing ourselves by driving off some shitty Iraqi highway. I'd been calm up until that point because I figured, if worse came to worse, I'd pop on the lights and we'd be fine—I'd just potentially get in trouble. So when I finally turned them on and nothing happened, it was a serious "oh shit" moment. We couldn't slow down because we were in the middle of the convoy. With deep culverts on either side of the highway, crashing off the side of the road at fifty miles-per-hour was a very real possibility. I was no longer able to make out the difference between the road and the desert—everything was black. We fell into a routine of Quinn shouting when we had gone too far to the right, while the grunt would shout when we had gone too far off the left. After what felt like the longest drive ever, we finally made it back to base in one piece. We almost ran into one of the barricades going through the maze in front of the FOB gate, but made it with no serious incidents. That was my first, and hopefully last, time driving. There have been a number of accidents due to guys either falling asleep or not being able to see well enough with the NVGs. The last way I'd want to die over here is by driving off the road because I can't see.

Outside Ar Rutbah, Iraq
October 5, 2004

Right now I'm sitting in the back of a Humvee at an OP outside of Ar Rutbah. I figured I would bring my journal along, so that I don't have to do these marathon sessions after we get back. We've finally switched to the three-day rotations for good, or so we've been told. I'm in the middle of a seventy-two hour MSR security mission at the moment. The word is that we're no longer going to conduct many raids or patrols into the city. From now on, we're supposed to primarily focus on patrolling Route Mobile. At this point, who really knows what's going on.

I'm not sure how I feel about sticking to MSR security the entire deployment. It would be somewhat similar to being kept on guard duty the entire tour. Necessary? Yes. But not exactly how I'd like to spend my tour. I don't consider myself to be some kind of gung ho maniac, but if I'm going to do this, then I may as well get some stories out of it. These longer periods outside the wire may make for easier logistics but they're way more tiring that shorter missions. By the end of three days out in the field, with only a little bit of scattered sleep, I'm pretty exhausted. Three days of sitting at OPs gets old real fast, and seems to

Sherman (left) and myself (right) resting at an observation post while not on guard duty.

leave me more tired than when we're actually doing something. That said, we were told that a supply convoy was hit by an ambush nearly an hour's drive east of Ar Rutbah. They received heavy fire, but were able to break through. We typically don't patrol that far east but it falls within our AO, so we may start. Not that it's a good thing, but it's nice to know that our mission does serve a purpose.

Camp Korean Village, Iraq
October 15, 2004

I received a few CDs from home—*The Killers* and *Modest Mouse*, all pretty good. It's nice just to have something new to listen to. If I would have known how much free time we would have in camp, then I would have brought more books and music. I also received a book about the British Empire, along with another that is a compilation of last letters home from German soldiers in World War I. The World War I book is pretty interesting; sad, but interesting. It's a little morbid, especially given where I am at the moment, to read other people's final letters before being killed. Some were written while guys were actually bleeding to death on the battlefield, knowing that they were about to die. Others were simply guys complaining about how they hadn't seen any action, only to die a couple days, or even hours, later. It was most interesting to see how the tone changed as the war dragged on. It went from excitement and eagerness to despair and resignation. In the beginning, they were ready to kick ass and take names, but by the end they all sounded like the living dead—knowing that their time was limited. Some had prepared letters in advance in case they died, but the majority were typical letters home that just happened to be their last. They often mention favorite memories such as lying in a field, or by a stream. It's somewhat telling that they focused on enjoyable, reflective moments spent in nature. Simple stuff, not the kind of thing you'd think would be your most precious memories. A couple mention memories from holidays or vacations, usually Christmas. Surprisingly, very little is mentioned about girls, although most were too young to be married.

Not that Iraq is anywhere close to the carnage of the Western Front, but those types of memories tend to be what I daydream about as well. Not the big parties at school, or the things I want to do when I get home—but the simple, relaxing things. I daydream about fishing by the river or walking around downtown in the evening. In general, not even specific events. Just a place, or a particular time of year. I've decided to write a last letter of my own, just in case. If I get home in one piece then I'll burn it. If not, then at least it tidies things up by offering family and friends a final goodbye. Although the book may be a little depressing, it's gotten me thinking. Not so much about death; rather, what I want out of life. It's almost like someone has hit the pause button on my life, so it's a good time to reflect on what I want to accomplish and whether I'm happy with what I've done thus far. That said, I still don't have the slightest idea. I've read histories about people who are described as having lived every minute to the fullest extent. I think, by our very nature, our dreams must always exceed our potential.

October 2004–January 2005:
Things Heat Up

Camp Korean Village, Iraq
October 26, 2004

On October 24, I came closer to death than I hope to ever get. Things had been ticking along fairly quietly in our AO and it was beginning to seem like we would have an uneventful deployment. Up until now, the only hostile action I've seen is the rocket attack shortly after we first arrived in Iraq, and the rare occasions when KV has been mortared. Occasionally the Muj set off an IED on one of our roving patrols, but so far my vehicle hasn't been targeted. And, to my knowledge, no vehicles in the AO have been hit directly since our arrival. So although I've heard a couple IEDs go off from a distance, the single riskiest event I've experienced remains the night drive back to KV without NVGs. Given how quiet things had been, I had started to think that mistakes like that, or sleepy drivers, would remain my biggest threats. But these last few days have reminded all of us that the city is full of people that would be more than happy to see us dead. Iraq may not be Vietnam or World War II, but that doesn't mean it's not a war zone.

I did nearly three back-to-back rotations outside the wire, for a total of eight days in the field. I was out with GG and the guys for the first rotation and on the second day out, we snagged two Hajjis riding a motorcycle. Military age males riding motorcycles have been on our BOLO list for the AO; apparently the Muj often use them to quickly zip away after setting off IEDs. While GG and the other guys stayed in the field, I was told to go with the grunts in taking the detainees back to KV. We loaded their motorcycle in the back of the Humvee and brought it and the two military age males back to base. Unintentionally, we smashed up their motorcycle as we were lowering it out of the back. Whoops. If those guys weren't insurgents before, they might be now that their ride looks like it's been beaten to hell. After that, I had a "day off" on base. It didn't end up being much of a day off. I spent the entire time with the other team at the makeshift rifle range just outside the base perimeter. We went through rotations shooting at the targets, including driving past the targets while shooting. It was actually decent training considering we haven't fired our weapons since we left the States.

When it came time for Sergeant Wallace's team to go out, instead of staying on KV to get back on my normal rotation, Wallace had me go with his team. I really didn't want to. Not because I didn't want to go outside the wire, but because I didn't want to somehow get permanently stuck on his team. Nothing against those guys, but I'm just used to my normal team. At this point, we know how each other operates. It's mainly the little things, like knowing when people aren't in the mood to joke around. Small stuff, but it makes a difference when you're spending every waking hour together. In the end, I'm glad that I did go with the other team—it was an active rotation with a good number of raids and patrols in and around the city. We left KV early in the morning of the first day out, stopping on top of a high mesa called OP Nipple to rally up for a raid. The OP got its name because it's the only feature sticking up out of an otherwise flat desert. When we got there it was still early, maybe around 0100, so we hopped out of the Humvees to sleep for a bit. I wouldn't have thought that I'd be able to sleep well on the cold ground without a sleeping bag, but it was the best rest I've had in a while. For whatever reason, the top of the mesa is covered in moon powder dust, similar to what the vehicles kick up on KV. That thick layer of dust made the ground feel nice and soft, almost cozy even.

We were awakened around 0400 when the other units arrived for the raid. We loaded up in the vehicles and raced down into the city. As part of the breach team, I rushed in on the target house and started hitting the door with the sledgehammer. After a couple hits, a guy inside the house just opened the door. That has happened before and it's always a bit comical—we're in the process of banging down the door, only to have a nervous looking Hajji hesitantly open it. We burst in and started clearing rooms, pulling everyone outside before checking each room in more detail. We found a couple AKs, which isn't unusual. One of the American translators kept demanding that the head of the household tell us how many weapons he had, but the guy kept denying having any more. Later, in their version of a living room, we pulled down a pile of pillows that were stacked up against a wall. Behind the pillows were a couple bolt-action hunting rifles while, at the same time, some of the grunts also found a handgun. The guns were old and clearly weren't weapons that an insurgent would use. Still, as punishment for lying to us the translator left the Hajji zip tied as we loaded back into the vehicles. Instead of leaving right away, we sat in the Humvees and waited for what seemed like an eternity. We were supposed to hit a second house but, after the delay, just ended up leaving. I don't think the higher-ups could figure out where exactly we needed to go. In all fairness, though we give them a lot of shit, the streets in this place are a complete maze. On top of that, it isn't like there are street signs or numbers. Making your way through this mess in the dark, even with a satellite image, is next to impossible.

The second day of the rotation was spent on MSR security. We primarily sat on the south side of the city, just south of a huge garbage dump. We had a good OP set up. We parked alongside a rocky out-cropping and arranged camouflage netting to cover our vehicles. A car driving down Route Mercury would never have been able to see us. We then had a couple guys climb on top of the rock outcropping in order to keep watch. If they saw a suspicious vehicle, they would then radio to a Humvee parked a half-mile down the road. We took turns as the team that was stopping vehicles and the one watching the road. The only downside was that the flies were out of control. They're bad everywhere but being near the dump must have com-pounded things. Allens had mosquito netting that he shared with whomever was on break. Still, it was hard to rest with fifty flies crawling all over you.

On the last day out with Wallace's team, we were called to help disable an IED that was found on Route Mobile. It was a long way east of the city, further than I've yet been. This was the first IED that I've seen up close and been able to walk around and examine. It was clearly built in order to hit one of our large supply convoys. The convoys are absolutely massive, miles and miles long. I've seen them rolling down Mobile while manning OPs at night—the headlights seem to go as far as the eye can see. After seeing the IED, the importance of our primary job of MSR security became very, *very* apparent. Evidently, LAR had seen the IED while they were on a roving patrol, so I guess we can no longer complain that the patrols don't serve a purpose. In total, the IED had twenty-eight artillery rounds in fourteen positions along the right side of the highway. Each position was roughly fifteen to twenty meters apart, so it stretched for nearly three hundred yards. Aside from the size, it was a textbook IED. Each artillery shell had its nose packed with semtex. Inserted into the semtex was a blasting cap with electrical wire that would detonate the shell. The wires ran to a central point where they were tied together—about one hundred meters from the road. That single wire then ran for nearly a half mile, to a spot behind a hill next to Route Michigan as it draws near, and parallel to, Mobile. It was a pretty simple setup. The insurgents could park behind the hill on Michigan and watch for a convoy. As soon as they saw one, they would send an electric charge down the wire, which would blow the blasting cap, which in turn would blow the semtex, which would then detonate the artillery shells. The Muj would be so far away that they would have been making their getaway down Michigan while the convoy was still trying to figure out what the hell had happened. An explosion of that size would have been massive. Imagine twenty-eight pieces of artillery firing at the same time, all hitting nearly the same point. With the stretch of road that the IED covered, there would have been no way that the Muj could have missed hitting at least one or two vehicles, if not more. We disassembled the IED, disconnecting the wires and removing the blasting caps. We then piled all the shells in the desert and blew them up. In retrospect, I can't understand why the insurgents didn't have the IED manned. At least I'm guessing that they didn't, since the LAR roving patrol drove into the middle of the IED before noticing it. It's possible that the Muj were watching but had assumed that the LAVs could withstand the blast. From what we've been told the insurgents are scared of the LAVs; they call them tanks, not knowing the difference.

So even though the initial raid had been a bust, between that and

The author kneeling beside a pair of artillery shells, components of a large IED found along Route Mobile. The device consisted of 28 shells, which were found and destroyed.

the big IED, it had already been an interesting rotation. It wasn't until the changeover that I found out that I wouldn't be going back to KV, but would be joining back up with my normal team of GG, Hayne, and Parrott. By that time, I had really been hoping that I wouldn't be staying out. I had spent five of the last six days outside the wire, so the idea of another three days wasn't appealing. Besides, my one "off day" had been spent on the rifle range. While we were driving to the rally point, a call came in that one of the engineers would be staying out. They couldn't say the name over the radio for security reasons, but they did say it was "Cpl Charlie," radio-speak for someone with a last name that begins with "C." Aside from Wallace, we had Allans, Burdette, Quinn, and myself—so A, B, Q, and D. Of course, it ended up being me. GG was giddy with schadenfreude as he came to get me.

On the first day of the third and final rotation, while on a roving patrol, the lead vehicle found yet another IED. Two days with back-to-back IEDs was previously unheard of in our AO. This one was found on Route Michigan, just east of the city. It was semi-buried in the ground alongside the road, across from a house that we call the Melon Farm. We radioed for EOD to come and blow it in place since we didn't want to risk disassembling it. The big IED on Mobile had been a different story, we could take it apart because we knew that it couldn't be set it off as we were disassembling it. But this one by the Melon Farm was too close to the city and in view of a couple of outlying villages. Also unlike the big one, the one by the Melon Farm was a wireless IED—so we couldn't trace it back to a firing position. This meant that the insurgents could have set it off from anywhere, as long as they had line of sight. We left before EOD blew it, but could hear the explosion from a distance. The second day was fairly quiet, more of the same— roving patrols and OPs. The last day of the rotation started out similarly. We spent the first part of the day driving around on a roving patrol with the infantry Captain, just his Humvee and ours. The HET guy rode in the back with Parrott and myself. We were visiting different houses in the area outside the city so that the HET guy could interview people. Most of our time was spent sitting in the Humvee keeping watch, while he and the Captain would go inside to chat. We were primarily on the east side of the city and first spent an hour at a house we call the Camel Farm. It's set back off of Route Michigan, so we didn't worry much about security and spent most the time messing with the camels and taking turns cleaning our rifles.

After the Camel Farm, we drove west on Michigan towards the city to visit the Melon Farm. Apparently the guy that lives there is a sheik, or so he claims, and the Captain wanted to see if he knew anything about the IED that was found across the street from his house. There seem to be enough people packed into every house in this country, it's likely that someone was home. Even if they weren't, it would have been hard not to notice a fresh hole dug in front of the house with a bomb half sticking out of it. We've stopped there a couple times before and the sheik has always been nice to us, giving us little watermelons—hence the name of his house. Not that that means he's not complicit, if not actively involved, in planting IEDs or keeping the Muj apprised of our whereabouts. After pulling up, we set up security outside of the house similar to before. The Captain's vehicle faced east down Michigan, while we were facing west in the direction of the city. The Melon Farm is much closer to the city, the majority of which is still out of view behind a hill, and is also much closer to the road than the Camel Farm, so we were a little more alert.

The Captain and HET guy hadn't been inside for more than fifteen minutes before a car came slowly driving down Route Michigan from the direction of the city. Michigan is a fairly busy road, especially at that time of day, so I didn't think much of it. Things have been so quiet here that a car driving slowly, though noticeable, didn't raise much suspicion. Suddenly, as it got a little closer, the car's tires squealed and it turned sharply off the road and sped straight towards us. Someone yelled "hey, hey," and I heard Parrott, who was on my left covering the road with the SAW (Squad Automatic Weapon), start firing. I was on the right side of the Humvee, the farthest side from the road, so I quickly jumped to the other side to get behind Parrott and started firing too. It all happened in a flash. As we fired, the vehicle's trajectory turned slightly to the right and began to arc back towards Michigan. As it swerved past, I could see blood on the driver. Even though I'd just cleaned my rifle while at the Camel Farm, it jammed after about five shots. But by that time it didn't really matter, the car had rolled past us and nearly come to a stop. It had essentially gone in a big "U" shape, off the road towards us and then back up—losing speed until it rolled

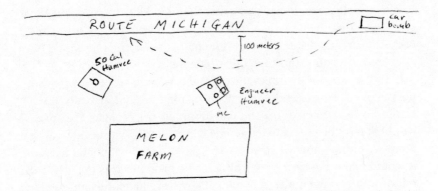

A sketch from the journal of the events of the suicide car bomb attack at the Melon Farm.

to a stop just to the side of Michigan. Parrott and I jumped out of the back of our Humvee and we all started setting up a perimeter around the area, with everyone moving as far away from the car as possible.

Things had gone from being just another uneventful, lazy day in a quiet corner of Iraq to full-on war zone mentality in just a few seconds. There was no need to discuss what had happened. Everyone knew that it was, without a doubt, a suicide car bomb. I called to Hayne, who was sitting in the driver's seat of the Humvee, to jump out and follow me to block traffic on Michigan. He looked a little stunned, as we all were. The Captain and HET guy came running out of the Melon Farm, with the Captain immediately calling for support over the radio. No longer even thinking about the car bomb, my immediate concern was of the potential for a follow-on attack. Expecting the car bomb to have killed half of us, it's not unlikely that the Muj would have had a force on standby to mop up any survivors from the initial blast. I was on edge until one of the squads of grunts arrived to back us up. By that time, I assumed any follow-on attack would have happened. The entire event felt like it occurred in slow motion, but was over in only a few moments—maybe ten or fifteen minutes from the initial attack to when support arrived. It's scary to think of how differently things could have gone. If Parrott wouldn't have been so quick on the trigger and killed the driver, then there's a good chance that we would have been killed. I'm sure one or two of my shots hit the bomber, since he rolled so close to our vehicle it would have been nearly impossible to miss. But those shots wouldn't have made a difference. At that point, he was almost certainly already dead or dying. If he hadn't been, then he would have triggered the bomb and I wouldn't be here.

In the ten minute interval from the car bomb attack to when support arrived, Hayne and I had been turning around a steady flow of traffic on Michigan. With the car bomb sitting so near the road, it wouldn't have been safe to let people drive alongside it. Besides, at that point we didn't know what was in the car, or just how much of a boom it would make. As we were turning traffic back towards the city, a car full of military age males drove up. They were laughing, smiling, and waving in a real friendly manner as they turned around; even giving me the thumbs up. By that point, it had been maybe two or three minutes since the suicide bomber struck us. I was still a little stunned and, if anything, was still on edge with the expectation of a follow-on attack. In retrospect, I should have stopped that car. There's a decent chance that those were the bomber's friends, either arriving for a follow-on attack or to see how their buddy had done. After seeing that the bomb hadn't gone off, they acted friendly and turned around. It's the only reason I can fathom for their strange behavior. Why else would a bunch of young guys be packed into a car, acting so bizarrely? From where we were directing traffic, they could clearly see an Iraqi car in the distance that had been shot to hell. The normal reaction of every other car was to curiously try and glimpse what had happened. Those first few minutes had been so chaotic that the Captain probably would have told us to just keep traffic moving. With only eight Marines in total, we didn't exactly have the manpower to secure the area, keep a wide perimeter away from the bomber's car, *and* start searching vehicles. Until help arrived, we were still in an exposed position. Still, it would have been good for the HET guy to have questioned them.

I still shudder thinking about how differently things could have played out. With only eight guys and the nearest help a ten minute drive away, if the bomb would have gone off then we could have easily been overrun by a follow-on attack. It's almost amazing that things like that don't happen more often. Maybe they do but the actual events are distilled to the simple headline: "Four Marines killed in Al Anbar province." Once support arrived and things became less tense, I walked to where our Humvee had been parked and picked up one of the empty bullet shell casings. Parrott had fired the majority of the rounds with the SAW, so I highly doubt that I picked up one that I had fired. In any case, it doesn't really matter. It's just something to show the future grandkids from the day granddad almost died in Iraq. Word must have spread quickly in the city because, after a while, traffic ceased to come down Michigan. More grunts arrived to take over the perimeter, so we killed time in the Humvee while waiting for EOD to arrive. After they did, EOD used their robot to inspect the car and take pictures. By this time it was dark and the Captain let us crowd around EOD's laptop to take a look at the images that the robot was picking up from inside the car. They found a few artillery shells, anti-tank shells, and landmines while suspecting that there were more in the trunk. That came as a relief to everyone. It's doubtful that we would have gotten into trouble considering the circumstances but, until it's confirmed hostile, you never know. The last thing I would want is to get some kind of disciplinary action for shooting up a civilian car.

It was deemed too risky to dismantle the bomb, so EOD walked up to the car to set a water charge underneath the driver's side to destroy it. I'm still not sure I understand the logic of that process. They use a robot to safely confirm that the car is full of explosive and, once they know that it is, they then walk up to set the charge? I guess there's no other way to do it, but that still doesn't make sense to me. Before they could set it off, the IPs (Iraqi Police) arrived and got into a heated argument about blowing up the car with the body inside. From the pictures the robot took, we could tell that it was a young guy in the driver's seat. It looked like blood had been gushing out of his mouth and chest. I'm guessing that there may be a religious issue with blowing apart the body, but it was disturbing to see the IPs—who are supposed to be on our side—so concerned with the body of a suicide bomber. He had just tried to kill us and was happy to be blown to pieces in the process. The Captain told the translator to let the IPs know that "They are very brave men, but that he can't let them risk themselves by trying to retrieve the body." I wouldn't have been surprised if they had knowledge of the bombing in advance. In any case, the Captain wouldn't budge and, after a brief delay, EOD blew up the car with the body still inside.

The explosion was intense—way more so than any of us had

expected and the car was absolutely obliterated. The explosion blasted the engine block up into the air, ultimately landing twenty-seven meters from where it had been. The shock wave from the blast knocked out power lines nearly two hundred meters away. Accompanying the blast and the flash of the power lines, was a metallic twang or buzzing sound as shrapnel flew overhead. We had assumed that we were parked far enough from the blast, but EOD had obviously underestimated how big it could be. That, or the trunk was loaded with much more explosives than anyone had anticipated. EOD and all the grunts were in hardback Humvees, but we were just sitting in the back of our unprotected high-back. We tensely sat for a few nervous moments as bits of debris landed around and behind us. It would have been darkly ironic if we had killed the driver of a VBIED, only to be wounded or killed hours later after setting it off ourselves.

After the explosion the Captain called for engineers to sweep the area for UXO, while the Iraqi Police swept the area to look for pieces of the body. The IPs had a blanket stretched out between four of them, picking up little pieces of the body and tossing them into the blanket. The three of us made our sweep for UXO but anything that could have exploded in the car had *definitely* gone off. We came across a length of the driver's spine, which we called for the IPs to come collect. It had chunks of meat still attached to it, but had otherwise been totally separated from any other parts of the body. By this time it was late, so we were doing our sweep in the dark with flashlights. As we were slowly walking and scanning, I obviously wasn't paying enough attention. I heard GG say "Davidson!" but it was too late, I had stepped on a chunk of meat from the bomber and my foot slid like I had stepped on a patch of ice. It would have been impossible to even venture a guess as to what part of his body it may have come from with the driver being so utterly destroyed in the blast. It sounds callous, but my first thoughts weren't of revulsion. I had, after all, just stepped on a piece of another human being—a piece that looked like something from the meat counter at a grocery store. I also wasn't struck by any highfalutin thoughts about the horrors of war, or that violence is something to be loathed. Instead, I was just annoyed at the thought that I would have to crawl into my sleeping bag with this stuff on the bottom of my boot. I wiped it off as best as I could and called the IPs over to pick it up.

On reflection, aside from the five to ten minutes of the attempted VBIED and the immediate aftermath, the whole episode felt procedural and was, by the end, actually boring. From start to finish we were probably stuck at the Melon Farm for six or seven hours and it felt much less dramatic than something from *Black Hawk Down*. As we were sitting around waiting, I couldn't help but think, "So this is modern combat"? IEDs and car bombs are my generation's version of the face-to-face battle lines of the Civil War or the Revolution. Parrott asked the Captain if we would get our combat action ribbons but was given a vague, non-answer as a response. Once everything was finished and EOD had left, we loaded up in the vehicles and moved to the Overturned Bus OP that is further from the city. I'm sure the Captain wanted to give us a break after the close call but, if anything, we wanted to go into the city. It finally feels like we're in a war and that there are people actively trying to kill us—clearly willing to die in the process. Of course we've known that the Muj are in the city, but IEDs and mortars feel so impersonal. A man driving a car packed full of explosives straight at you is as personal as it gets. They want to kill us and we want to fight back. Sounds simple, but in this kind of war it's just not that easy. We wouldn't know where to go to find the enemy and, even if we did, they probably wouldn't oblige us by fighting.

Fortunately we changed over with the other team the next morning at 0600, because I didn't sleep much on the last night. I must have still had some adrenalin going but by the time we got back to base, it had dissipated and I felt completely drained. Doing eight days of the last nine outside the wire also probably had something to do with it. It wasn't until late that last night in the field, while I was on watch, that it really hit me just how close we had come to being killed. The car had been ten feet away before the driver slumped to the side and it started curving back towards the road. There are a lot of what-ifs. *What if* the driver hadn't slumped to the right—the car may have rolled into us and the jolt could have set off the bomb. *What if* Parrott hadn't grabbed the SAW when we changed over—I'm not sure that M16s alone would have been able to stop the car in time. *What if* we hadn't cleaned our weapons, which really needed it, while waiting at the Camel Farm. On top of those what-ifs, EOD said that the bomber had a suicide switch under his foot and one in his hand. So, even though the driver was dead, the bomb should have gone off when he released the pressure on either of those switches. It's not worth thinking about, and I suppose it wasn't all luck. We chose to clean our weapons and Parrott chose to grab the SAW. He's been hard to get to know, but he's definitely a good Marine. I'm not sure that most of the other guys in our squad would have been ready to fire the moment the car's tires squealed. I've got to give him credit, he saved our lives.

The officers always emphasize the importance of not getting complacent, "complacency kills" is even painted on the walls around the FOB. This attack has been testament to the importance of staying alert. But still, it's hard not to get complacent in this place. Unless we're on a raid, it feels like we do the same things day in and day out. Driving up and down the same roads, sitting at the same OPs, and even raiding the same houses. I guess we have been getting complacent, or at least I have been. Until now, this area just hasn't been in "full-blown war" mode. It's felt more like we're police, parked on the side of the road to keep an eye on traffic. It's hard to stay focused for long periods of time while doing tedious, monotonous patrols and OPs. As strange as it may sound, we would probably be a bit safer if we had a higher probability of being attacked—it would keep us more alert. Due to our posture in the area, if the bomber would have slowly driven up and waived or motioned to speak with us, instead of speeding his car straight at us, then there's a good chance that we would have let him get close enough for the bomb to have done some serious damage. Hajjis often drive up to us in order to give information, or to try to talk to us. We don't let them get too close but with the size of that bomb it wouldn't have mattered.

Suicide bombings are hard for me to wrap my head around. Even tonight, I haven't been able to shake that eerie feeling. What would possess someone to willingly kill themselves in the hope of taking some of us with him? If I was an insurgent, I could understand taking shots at us—in a way I can respect it. But I don't understand what could possess someone to drive down the road, knowing that he was going to die in just a couple minutes. To not even have the chance to live to fight another day. From the pictures taken by the robot, I could tell that the driver was only in his early or mid-twenties. I get nervous when I have a test in school that I'm unprepared for, I can't imagine waking up in the morning with the knowledge that I won't live to see the following day. There is so much in life that I still want to do, still want to accomplish. It seems unimaginable to make the willing choice to die. Before shipping out, I read an interview with a guy that had volunteered to be a suicide bomber. He seemed so absurdly, over-the-top committed to his cause that I just assumed it was a publicity stunt by an insurgent group. We've been told that bombers are often recruited from people who have fallen on hard times. In exchange for volunteering, the Muj promise to take care of their families. If true, it speaks to just how hard some of these people's lives must be. From a political or military perspective, the bomber must have known that, even if he killed all four of us, it wouldn't have had much of an impact, if any. Bush wouldn't suddenly issue orders to pull out of Iraq. Essentially, the driver was willing to die in the hope that, in aggregate, enough violence will eventually send the U.S. packing. Killing us *might* make the population back home a modicum more agitated about ending the war. But in reality, it would have been just another brief headline scrolling on the CNN news ticker. The only lasting impact would have been the devastation that it would have wrought on our families.

Afterwards, when we had a chance to bullshit about what had happened, most of the guys were understandably pissed at the driver. I suppose it's a normal response to be angry with someone who has tried to kill you, but I don't feel any emotion towards him at all. If anything, I feel slightly sorry for him. He's dead now, not having made a difference of any kind. Right now, he could be sitting at home with his family. Instead, he's been blown to little pieces and collected in a blanket. The world, and the war, continue on. I also don't feel as if we've made much of a difference in killing him. One less guy that wants to kill us, but there's plenty more where he came from. I guess that's what really puzzles me about suicide bombers. In the news a suicide bombing sounds sensational, which is the point. In reality, a bombing off the side of some dirty road in middle-of-nowhere Iraq seems as far removed from global, geopolitical events as can be. This place couldn't be further from the decision-makers in Congress, yet that's the sphere of power that the Muj are trying to influence. The ground-level reality is that one minute we were all sitting in the Humvee, the bomber drove at us, was killed, and we went back to sitting in the Humvee. If he would have succeeded then our families would have been upset. But, whether he succeeded or not, one little event involving a half dozen people has zero impact in the overall scheme of things.

On reflection, I'm happy with my response to the attack. I was covering my area and, when I saw the threat, I didn't hesitate to fire. That had been a big mental hurdle. We've always been told that you never know how you'll react until you're thrust into that kind of situation. I didn't have time to assume that Parrott had already killed the driver, so I fired with the intent to kill. Afterwards I felt excited and confident and was quick to set up a perimeter and get ready for a follow-on attack. It'll be interesting to see how this changes our posture in the AO. Until now, it has been a reasonably quiet zone. We had heard reports that large numbers of Hajjis had been coming into town, fleeing from the impending attack on Fallujah. Recent events would seem to point to the intel guys being right. In the last few days we've found two well placed IEDs and been targeted by a car bomb. I'm sure we'll follow up with the sheik at the Melon Farm. An IED in front of his house on one day, followed by a car bomb a couple days later. We hadn't been there long enough for the Muj to have seen us and gotten the bomb ready. It's more likely that someone in that house called, setting the attack into motion.

Camp Korean Village, Iraq
October 31, 2004

The most recent three-day cycle seemed to pick up where the last one had left off. On the first night outside the wire we went to chat with the Goat Man. I carried the radio for the Captain, so was able to listen to the conversation. The Goat Man told us to expect more car bombs, which wasn't something we wanted to hear. Everyone dislikes the idea of VBIEDs much more than IEDs, and certainly more than being ambushed or mortared. His warning put us all on edge. He also told us that the insurgents were planning to hide bombs in motorcycles with sidecars, which sounded strange since I haven't seen many motorcycles since we've been here. In fact, I don't think I've ever seen one with a sidecar. In the classes we received prior to deploying, we were told that the Muj usually make suicide car bombs from vehicles that are nondescript and won't attract much attention. I don't think a motorcycle with a sidecar fits that profile. Even so, the Goat Man was spot-on with some of his intel. The day after we spoke with him, a convoy of LAR escorting the water truck from the pumping station back to KV was hit by a car bomb. It wasn't a motorcycle; instead, it was a car that looked like the mirror image of the one that had targeted us. The convoy was driving west on Mobile, back to base, when a car sped up and rammed the last LAV in the column. For some reason the bomb didn't go off, so the car sped up again and rammed the next vehicle in line, which was the water truck, but it still didn't detonate. Finally the LAR guys were able to shoot the bomber as he was attempting to drive towards the next vehicle in the convoy.

We were at an observation post near the city when the attack went down. When the call came in over the radio, we raced west on Mobile and were one of the first to arrive to help secure the area. The suicide car had been riddled with bullets and crashed into a ditch on the eastbound side of Mobile. We quickly drove past it in order to stop traffic coming down the highway. After the size of the explosion from the last car bomb, we widened the size of the cordon around this car so that we were nearly ¼ mile away. We also couldn't let traffic pass on Mobile as it would come too near the bomb. I was with Naseem the translator, trying to calm down a group of truck drivers that wanted to go around on the westbound lanes of the highway. There was no way we could let them try and, after a while, they gave up arguing and attempted to turn around. Unfortunately, the second one that tried popped his tires on the median and was stuck, blocking the way for all the others. It took a long time for EOD to arrive from KV, by which time the traffic jam on Mobile was massive.

EOD didn't bother with the robot this time, there was no uncertainty around the fact that it was another car bomb. The HET guy really wanted to inspect the body, since he hadn't been able to look at the last one, so EOD decided to dismantle the car bomb and detonate all of the explosives in the desert. It was decided that, if EOD was going to approach the vehicle, they wanted to be absolutely sure that the driver was dead. So we had to wait for one of the LAR guys to shoot the driver from a distance a few more times. Afterwards EOD approach and once they gave us the OK, we joined them to help disassemble the bomb. It seemed to be similar to the one that had targeted us. The car was packed with six 160mm mortar rounds, six 155mm artillery rounds and six anti-tank landmines. It was an absolutely massive bomb, with about half of the payload in the trunk and the other half spread around the floor of the car. After EOD took the blasting caps out from each of the shells and anti-tank mines, we helped stack everything a few hundred yards into the desert. Out of curiosity, I hung around the HET guy as he searched the body. Again, it was a male in his early to mid-twenties and I was surprised to find a bunch of folded papers stuffed in the breast pocket of his man-dress. I'll have to follow up with the HET guy after he gets them translated. If I had to guess, I would assume that they are religious messages—I'm not sure what else a suicide bomber would carry when expecting to be blown to pieces.

I took a picture of the body, both because the HET guy wanted some documentation and also to satisfy my own morbid curiosity.

The contents of a car bomb used in an attempted attack on an LAR convoy.

Aside from a stream of blood coming from his mouth and spots of blood on his clothes, he didn't really look dead. Despite being shot a number of times the only telltale sign that he was dead was his ashen appearance. The HET guy dragged the body around in a very uncere- moniously way as he searched it—chucking it down into the ditch. After EOD had blown the explosives and we finished one last look through the car, the HET guy made a point of flipping the body over to leave it face down in the dirt. Traffic had finally started moving again on Mobile and he said he wanted the steady stream of trucks creeping by to see the bomber face down in a ditch. Even before the last couple rotations, the HET guy had struck me as being a little odd. After the car bomb that nearly hit us, one of the grunts said that he saw the HET guy walk up and tap the driver on the head with his pistol to "make sure he was dead"—which he clearly was. It's possible that Iraq is getting to him, this is his second tour and HET is a stressful job. He mentioned being jittery and nervous when he went home between tours, not able to relax when going out with friends. I don't personally care how he treated the body, but it struck me as strange. Maybe I just haven't seen enough dead people to be properly desensitized.

We hadn't even left the scene before the Iraqi Police arrived to pick up the body. Considering we had stopped traffic going in both directions on Mobile, I'm not sure how they even knew about the attack—which seemed, yet again, suspicious. That night we went back to speak with the Goat Man. As we waited for the Captain and HET guy, we could hear AK and machine gun fire in the city. The Goat Man told them that the local men of Ar Rutbah were fighting recently arrived insurgents who had staked out a spot in the eastern side of the city. The rumor that has been circulating is that the new Iraqi police chief is serious about cleaning up the city but given what we've seen on the last couple rotations, I have my doubts. At any rate, something is clearly going on in the city because the Captain confirmed that the shooting wasn't coming from any of our units. I suppose I've never considered it before, but it is a little surprising to think that the Iraqis fight amongst themselves to the same degree as they fight us—using machine guns and bombs. What a violent place. I suppose it's a little like the Hatfield and McCoy feud. In a lawless place like this "might equals right," so they use every tool at their disposal.

That night, the Goat Man gave us the descriptions of two car bombs that he was aware of, one which matched the car that attempted to hit the LAR convoy. The other was the motorcycle that he had mentioned the previous night. Considering that his shack doesn't have power and is a long walk from the city, I'm guessing he hadn't yet heard about the day's attack. If that's the case and he's not knowingly feeding us news that we already know, then I really hope we're paying him well—this kind of intel is priceless. He also told us that the Muj leaders are planning a big regional meeting and, if we were willing to pay, he could find out the details. The Captain and HET guy seemed to think that he's simply trying to milk us for money but, so far, he seems legit. The last time we spoke to him he made a fair point about money. Basically, he can either wander around town talking to people and getting information, or he can try to get work. Either way, he's going to need money to feed his family. Besides, I don't think it really costs us much. He also told us that if he's able to find out the location of the big meeting, he would be willing to ride in a Humvee and point it out. Those don't sound like the actions of someone who is only concerned about squeezing us for every dollar.

The next day was fairly quiet, with just standard MSR security. While on roving patrols everyone was extra alert but there were no more attacks. Once the sun went down we went back to see the Goat Man. I sat in the back of the Humvee while the Captain, HET guy, and translator went inside. There was another bout of fighting between the Hajjis on the east side. As I sat in the Humvee looking at the lights of the city, I saw the flash of an IED—quickly followed by two more. The first explosion was accompanied by a flurry of AK fire, which reached a crescendo after the second and third IEDs. In a strange way it was almost soothing to lounge in the back of the Humvee with my feet up on the bench, watching the fight. When muffled by distance, explosions and shooting create a unique soundtrack. I'd see a flash and, after a two or three second delay, would hear the accompanying boom. We still don't have any clarity as to what exactly is going on in the city. Earlier today we were told that the fighting may not even be related to the insurgency. There's a good chance that it may just be rival smugglers or family clans fighting for control. I can't help but wonder at how many Iraqis have died over the centuries in the unending fight for dominance. Even in this desolate place, with mile after mile of uninterrupted nothingness, people fight and murder each other for the chance to be top dog. It's a country with a long history and before there were IEDs and AKs, they used swords and spears. The upside of winning is what? A slightly nicer house and a little more money than your neighbors. I know it's condescending since it wasn't too long ago when America was the same way, but I still can't wrap my head around it. In any case, I'd say that it's unlikely to be the Iraqi Police taking the Muj to task. If they were actually going to fight the insurgents and things were getting that heated, they would call us for help.

The Goat Man didn't have any other news for us and, since he was told that we can only pay him *after* his intel leads to a kill or capture, he's decidedly less enthusiastic. It's understandable. Why put yourself and family at risk if it may not pay? He also mentioned that people are growing suspicious of him. Someone visiting his house earlier in the day asked about the number of boot prints in the sand. Later in the day, a passenger in a car threw a grenade in the direction of his house while driving by. If the Muj seriously suspected him of being an informer, then they would do much more than toss a grenade near his house. So it may have just been meant as a simple warning, letting him know that he's being watched—not a good thing for him or us. The Captain promised to bring him a radio, an AK, and an infrared strobe that can be used to get our attention in case of emergency.

We changed over the next morning after a rainy, chilly night. We were told that KV had been mortared fairly heavily the day before but that no one had been hurt. We were also informed that the higher-ups want to start sending patrols out each night in order to hunt for the Hajjis that have been mortaring the base. I think a couple of OPs would do the trick. It seems obvious that the Muj must be firing their mortars from either Routes Mobile or Silver—the only two roads within range of our base. Patrolling around the desert won't do anything. If they were shooting from the desert, then the helicopters that lift off as part of the react force after each mortar attack would have found them. It's more likely that they pull off the road, fire, then throw everything back into the car and drive away. We were also told that because of the second car bomb attack, we are now allowed to shoot at the tires of any cars that get too close to us. Prior to this change we were supposed to follow a series of steps that build up from waving or firing a flair, before we actually shoot at the car. This change may end up backfiring if we shoot at every civilian car that accidentally gets too close. The other team already fired on a car while driving from KV to the changeover. That said, although no one has been killed yet, I'll always err on the side of safety. One of the grunts told us that eight Marines were recently killed by a car bomb in Fallujah. If true, then it highlights the seriousness of what happened to us the other day.

After returning from the last rotation I heard that the Red Sox won the World Series. I had watched every minute of the playoffs last year, but this year it hasn't even crossed my mind. I guess I'll have to wait another eighty-something years to see it for myself. We may be going back out again on a raid tonight but are still waiting to hear. I hope not, I need a break.

Camp Korean Village, Iraq
November 1, 2004

We're going out again this evening on a raid. We haven't been told whether the target is in the city, or somewhere else. Both teams have been hitting some isolated houses and truck stops recently—supposed waypoints for foreign fighters moving into the country. The tone and posture in our AO has definitely taken a distinct turn. Everyone is more alert, amped up, and on guard. It's no longer hyperbole, people's lives really are on the line. I wouldn't expect for this pace of attacks to continue for the next four to five months without taking casualties at some point. Our teams can only get lucky but so many times.

I paid a visit to the computer center this morning and had a chance to talk to people back at school on IM. The chatter and gossip is the same as always, not that I would expect anything different. Everything people talked about seemed so petty when compared to what's going on here. It's almost like people find ways to be discontent, even though they should be enjoying the best years of their lives. Still, it was nice to hear that I'm missed. I would obviously expect my absence to be felt by family, but it's always difficult to tell with friends. I nearly expected them to seamlessly move on without me, barely noticing. I also gave my parents a call and it sounds like everyone is doing fine, so I'm now caught up with everyone. I told Dad that nothing has been happening in our AO. I had debated telling him the truth but I'm glad I didn't, I could tell that he was happy not to know too much. I had barely gotten the words out, explaining that it's been boring and quiet, before he said "oh, that's good to hear" like a weight had been lifted off his shoulders. It strikes me that we haven't heard from the other guys in our platoon for quite a while. Initially we had been hoping for weekly updates but, as far as I know, we've only be in touch a couple times since leaving Al Asad.

Camp Korean Village, Iraq
November 10, 2004

The last rotation was a bit shorter as we only went outside the wire for sixty hours. Since the car bomb attack, the infantry Captain thinks we're hot shit—so now we've been going wherever he goes. Since he needs to be wherever there is the highest likelihood of action, we have a good chance of seeing more ourselves. Although not prudent, I suppose it's better than spending day after day on guard duty or something equally as boring. On the first night out on this last rotation, the Captain's Humvee was targeted by an IED at the corner of Routes Phoenix and Michigan, on the west side of town. Fortunately, no one was hurt as it was delayed and exploded after they had rolled pass. This was one of the few instances when we weren't with him. He had just dropped us off at a spot near the city where we set up an OP for the night, while he went with one of the infantry squads to do a quick roving patrol around the area. I was scheduled to have watch at 0200 so by the time the IED went off, I had already gotten in my bag and fallen asleep. It was probably just a standard IED but we weren't far away so the explosion sounded massive, it seemed to reverberate through the ground.

At first I didn't really know what had happened. I was still groggy when I jumped out of my bag and, for some reason, my first thought was that it had been an earthquake. I was half asleep and said to someone "there's been an explosion or something" which brought a few "no shit" responses. There wasn't much we could do but sit around the radio and wait to hear if there had been any casualties. Luckily no one was hurt and the Captain made his way back to our OP while the infantry squad set up their own a little to the southeast of us. Not more than an hour later, the infantry squad opened up with a machine gun on a car that had driven up to their position. They must have been a little nervous after the IED and the recent car bomb attacks. So I jumped awake again, this time to see tracers flying through the night sky just off to our left. I thought that we were under attack and I had a moment of panic before realizing what was happening. The last place I would want to be during the start of an attack is curled up in my sleeping bag.

The next day was uneventful, with the standard MSR security routine: roving patrols, vehicle checkpoints, and manning OPs. That night we did a foot patrol to the Routes Phoenix and Michigan intersection where the Captain had been IEDed the night before. It has become a common spot for IEDs. The insurgents keep dropping new ones into the crater, so now there's a huge hole on the side of the road. It's tough to see inside the crater from the vehicle until we're almost on top of it, which makes it a good spot on a busy intersection to keep hitting us. They can also observe the intersection from deeper inside the city, which makes it low risk for the triggerman. Since we can't get the triggerman, the only one at risk is the poor sucker they pay to drop the IED by the side of the road. Intersections are a favorite target for the Muj as we naturally slow down while making the turn. The only downside from the insurgents' perspective, is that the deeper the crater gets, the less effective the IED.

There were only six of us on the foot patrol and, although we had help nearby if we needed it, it was probably the first time I've actually been somewhat scared while on a patrol. If things went sideways, six people aren't enough to hold it together very long—even if help is nearby. This intersection has come to represent the front line between the insurgent-held city, and our heavy presence on the roads and highway just outside the city. They know we usually set up OPs along the Michigan/Ski intersection or in the Triangle, so if they were going to drop off another IED then they would definitely be alert and armed. We set up a little observation post behind a shack that must be a butchers shop because it stunk like rotting meat. The combination of that smell, along with the ever-present Iraqi city smell of diesel fuel and dog shit, made for a miserable night.

At one point a group of young guys walked near us and cheerfully said "hi," like we were friends passing on the street. I can't put my finger on the reason, but it made me feel somewhat embarrassed. Here we are, running around at all hours of the night playing war while most the people are just trying to get on with their daily lives. This would feel more like a war if it were a nearly abandoned city, reduced to rubble—probably like Fallujah is now. Instead it's still a bustling city. Most people just ignore us as we run around on patrols. While we're leap frogging positions, ducking and taking cover—they stand around watching and drinking tea. It all feels a little silly. At least until something actually happens, then you remember that you're doing all this for a reason.

The night patrol/OP ended uneventfully and we made our way back out of the city to set up an OP in the Triangle. The remainder of the rotation was fairly quiet, with the exception of one of our OPs being mortared. That was a first, as far as I know. The Muj usually don't mortar OPs since we don't stay in one spot for very long. The rounds impacted but only about half exploded, which is odd since they *definitely* know how to fire mortars. We've been told that the mortar shells may have been gas projectiles and that the insurgents didn't know the difference and therefore didn't fire them properly to disperse the gas. It is pure speculation, but I hope they never figure out the difference. From the little I've read about World War I, a gas attack is one way I really don't want to die. If they are able to confirm it, then the higher-ups will probably make us start to carry our gas masks again—which is a pain in the ass. After the mortars hit, we drove around the desert looking for the firing position but, of course, couldn't find it. I'm starting to wonder about our leadership. It seems obvious that the Muj wouldn't leave the city and go into the surrounding desert—where we have all of our OPs and roving patrols—to fire their mortars. They can fire from somewhere in the city where we have almost no presence except for the occasional raid or patrol. They can take their time and, in all reality, could spend a half hour in one place before we could finally get to them.

Despite this somewhat quiet rotation, it still seems like things are heating up. Not too long ago a rotation out in the field with an IED attack and an OP being mortared would have been unheard of. Everyone seems more anxious. We all know that we can't keep getting IEDed, car bombed, or mortared each rotation without eventually taking casualties. After getting back to KV we were told that we are now required to wear flak jackets and helmets while on base. Apparently KV was hit by seven mortars yesterday, with some of the rounds actually impacting inside the perimeter. Today, during chow, KV was mortared yet again. I was stupid and took the heavy SAPI (Small Arms Protective Inserts) plates out of my flak jacket while on base, since I figured I wouldn't need them. I don't think I'll be doing that again. I feel childish at having taken them out in the first place. It was something of a silent protest at having to wear flak jackets at all while on base, which everyone finds unnecessary. As we were mortared during chow, the Captain and the guys that ride in his vehicle were rushing out of the chow hall to load up and search for the mortar men. He yelled for us to come with him, so we quickly grabbed our stuff and ran to catch up. I felt naked being outside the wire without the plates in, even though we didn't come across anything. Still, how stupid would it have been if something had happened and I was caught without the plates?

We've been told that the attack on Fallujah has started in earnest and that the higher-ups expect a large number of insurgents to move into our AO as Fallujah and Ar Rutbah share familial ties. Apparently 1st Platoon from our Charlie Company has been attached to an infantry battalion that is leading the way in Fallujah. We were also told that once things in Fallujah settle down and they are able to get more troops our way, the higher-ups plan to repeat the process in other cities across Al Anbar. Eventually, they plan to cordon off Ar Rutbah and send us all into the city to do a mini version of what's going on now in Fallujah. If clearing the insurgents out of Ar Rutbah is actually an objective that the higher-ups want to achieve, then that would probably be the only way to do it. Otherwise the insurgents will always run the show and we'll continue to only control the roads and highway outside the city. Frankly, I would be surprised if we ended up doing it. Controlling this city wouldn't be worth the time, money, effort, and potential casualties. Once the Iraqi government is up on its own two feet, then they may need to do something to gain a degree of control over the city—but there really wouldn't be any benefit to us now.

I haven't been able to contact home in a while. At first the phone center was having technical issues and now it's been completely shut down because of the ongoing operation in Fallujah. Apparently they don't want us passing info home, not that we know anything that's classified. There's a good chance that the people at home have more recent, accurate knowledge of what's going on than we do. I miss talking to people at home, especially Mom and Dad. It's nice to get mail, but it's not the same as actually hearing someone's voice.

Camp Korean Village, Iraq
November 15, 2004

This last rotation outside the wire was the most exciting, if that's the right word, to date. We started the first day of the three-day rotation with one of the infantry squads instead of with the Captain. On the first day we set up an OP on the east side of the city. Later that day we moved to the southeast side, which is an area that we typically ignore because there are only a few dirt roads leading in and out of the city from that direction. We were situated on a hill just over a quarter of a mile from the edge of the city, so quite a distance away, and we hadn't been there long before a sniper started taking pot shots at the OP from the city. Apparently the grunts observed him as he propped his rifle on the hood of his car and began firing. Our Humvee was watching the six (rear), so we didn't come under this initial fire. After it started, the grunts called us over the radio and we rushed over, jumping out of the Humvee to set up a firing line along the ridge of the hill. The sniper was firing from a good eight hundred meters away and his closest shot impacted about twenty meters short of us, pretty damn good given the distance. We didn't return fire. It would have taken a very good shot from an M16 to hit him from that distance and, odds are, we would have only ended up hitting some poor civilian's house. He fired three shots, although I only saw the impact of the final one. After his last shot, he hopped into his car and tried to drive away. Evidently the car wouldn't start, so he and another guy jumped out to push. At first we thought that this presented the perfect opportunity to nab them, so we loaded up into the vehicles in order to race down into the city. We called it in to the Captain but he told us to hold off, thinking that it might be a trap to lure us into an ambush. We waited for the Captain to arrive and, by the time he showed up, the sniper had already cleared out. I didn't think about it at the time, but in retrospect it seems like they may have been testing our reaction time. By popping off a few shots from a safe distance, they could then wait to see how long it would take for support to arrive. In any case, even though it was frustrating at the time, considering how the rest of the rotation turned out, the Captain probably made a good call.

After the excitement we detached from the infantry squad and joined the Captain. We set up an OP for the night on the east side of Phoenix, among some rock piles and an unfinished house foundation across from the Triangle. It was a nerve-racking night. We heard a lot of shots and commotion coming from the city. It almost sounded like fireworks, which it may have been. The lights from the city completely blinded our night vision so we couldn't see anything and, for some reason, the thermal sights weren't working either. The Muj could have walked right up to me from the direction of the city and I wouldn't have been able to see them until they were on top of us. It was almost like having nobody on watch at all. When you can hear nearby gunfire, it makes for a very long night. Luckily, the only bad thing that happened was that Parrott took a shit near the back of the Humvee which most of us ended up stepping in. Apparently, he thought we would be moving to a different OP before settling in for the night.

The next day, we stayed put along the western edge of the city in the Triangle that's formed by Routes Phoenix, Michigan and Ski. We had set up a vehicle checkpoint for cars coming off of Mobile, heading down Phoenix towards the city. We put a road block team, just two or three guys with cones, at the point of the triangle where Route Ski connects with Phoenix. The road block team was to direct any black BMWs coming down Phoenix off onto Ski. From there, a search team would go through the vehicles and question the passengers. We kept up the searches well into the afternoon with each of us taking turns on either the roadblock team, the search team, manning a M240G which was positioned to overlook Ski, or taking a rest at the OP in the Triangle.

While I was sitting next to our Humvee taking a break, I noticed a guy in black standing out in the desert a few hundred yards west of Ski. Typically, it wouldn't have raised any suspicion since shepherds let their flocks wander all over the desert to eat up the little bits of grass. But this guy was just standing there, watching us—with no other indication of why he would be there. We called to the Captain and were told to keep an eye on him. After ten minutes, the guy simply walked down to Route Michigan where a car zipped over to pick him up. Having someone so blatantly scoping out our position made the hairs on my neck stand up. From that point on, all the normal chatter and joking ceased. We all felt the tension, knowing that it would only be a matter of time before something happened. I overheard the Captain mention that he was surprised we hadn't been mortared yet. Given that an OP had been mortared on the last rotation, it seemed to be the most likely scenario. I was OK with mortars and was just hoping that we wouldn't be car bombed. He also mentioned that we were in a good place if we were attacked, so there was a certain degree of intention on his part in deciding to set up in the Triangle. Around 1600, the tension finally broke as the anticipate attack finally got underway. In a sense, it actually came as a relief. But instead of a mortar attack, or even another car bomb, it was a carefully planned ambush.

The Muj came towards us from the direction of the city, taking up positions behind the piles of stone building material where we had set up our OP the night before. It was a well-planned attack; by coming from that direction, they were able to stay behind the cover of the hill and get into positions near us without being noticed. At the time, I was manning the M240G on the western side of Route Ski. Perhaps I'm giving the insurgents too much credit, but they launched their attack with perfect timing as well. Just as they attacked, GG and Sherman had started to walk down the hill to begin searching a vehicle that Parrott and Hayne had directed down Ski. At that moment I heard a loud snap. Then another, and then another. It sounded exactly like rounds going overhead when pulling targets at the rifle range. At first I felt a slight panic, not because I was scared of the fight, but because I didn't know where the shooting was coming from. I was lying flat on the ground, manning the gun and spinning in circles trying to identify a target. My first thought was that the Muj may be attacking from the desert to our west, where we had seen their scout, but that didn't make any sense. Then I looked south, towards the bombed-out hospital at the base of the triangle along Route Michigan. I'm not sure why I thought they would attack from there, except that it seems like the ideal place. It's a large building that looks like something out of Stalingrad, after having been bombed in the early days of the 2003 invasion. The Muj could move all over the building and egress relatively easily. But our training really does work, I fought against every instinct that screamed to just fire at something by reminding myself that I shouldn't fire until I've identified a good target.

The civilians in the vehicle that GG and Sherman were planning to search jumped out and hid in a ditch next to route Ski with Thomas, our Sudanese translator—confirming that they weren't part of the attack. I was in an exposed position on top of the western embankment of Route Ski and think that one of the Muj must have been shooting directly at me; I could hear rounds snapping overhead like a scene from *Black Hawk Down.* But the main portion of their fire seemed to be directed at the Captain's hardback Humvee that has the .50 cal. I saw a number of shots kicking up dirt around it, and saw the Captain duck down while he was reporting the ambush on the radio from the protected passenger side.

The amount of time spent searching for the source of the ambush was, in reality, only fifteen to twenty seconds. Fifteen or twenty seconds may even be an exaggeration, it could have been less but felt like an eternity. The Muj finally exposed their position when they fired an RPG, probably directed at the Captain's Humvee, which flew over us and blew up in the desert behind us. I'm not sure what I expected, but the RPG didn't look very menacing as it flew through the air. It was glowing red and looked harmless, like a large roman candle. But I didn't actually see it impact and to be honest, I can't even remember hearing it. GG told me afterwards that it made a good sized explosion in the desert behind us. Now knowing where they were, I turned the 240G towards the direction of fire but couldn't open up because our guys in the Triangle were in my line of sight. I picked up the M240G and ran down the embankment onto Route Ski and back up the other side, into the Triangle. I stopped at our Humvee to dump the M240G and grab the SAW, which had more ammo and would be easier to carry and fire.

I must admit, I felt pretty pumped as I ran towards the firing. Thomas was hiding in the ditch with the vehicle passengers and was cheering as I ran past. I had a brief burst of adrenalin and thought "now we're finally going to go toe-to-toe with these guys." It felt like we've been dancing around each other with the occasional raid, mortar attack, or IED; but now we were going to really fight. That feeling faded quickly after I exchanged weapons at our Humvee. I hadn't run far and I consider myself to be in decent shape, but I felt like I just couldn't get enough air. I was gasping for breath, just like the first time I got into a boxing ring. The combination of excitement and fear sapped my energy much more than a typical run, even when carrying a twenty-five pound weapon.

After I picked up the SAW, I joined GG and Sherman who had rushed up from Route Ski as well. They both went straight towards the top of the embankment overlooking Route Phoenix, while I curved to the right towards the Captain's Humvee. The insurgents were on the other side of Phoenix from us and I could feel the shots snapping over

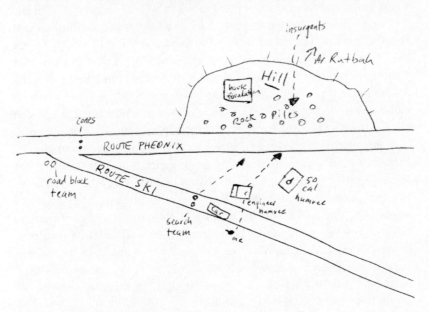

A sketch from the journal of the events of the ambush at the Triangle, on the west side of Ar Rutbah.

my head as the Marine in the turret of the Captain's Humvee returned fire from above and behind me. By this point we were finally in a good position to close on them, which they must have known because they began to immediately disengage. I fired a short burst from the SAW but didn't have a good target, just a general idea of the direction in which they were crawling away from brief flashes of movement. As the ambush came to an abrupt end, it was both a disappointment and relief. There were only six of us in total in the Triangle, with a couple more not far away. Based on what we found afterwards, the Muj had at least that many, if not more. It was a very vulnerable feeling. Even with all of America's military might and firepower, it they had pushed their advantage they could have possibly overrun us before help could arrive. At the end of the day we were actually well matched in terms of firepower. They had AKs, RPGs, and a light machine gun while we had our rifles, the SAW, and the .50 cal. But, if they had been able to close on us quickly, even the 50 cal. wouldn't have helped.

After they disengaged, one of the infantry squads arrived to our south and started doing fire-team rushes forward. I found out after the fact that while we were being attacked, the Captain was calling in this squad of grunts. They were ordered to drive down Route Michigan and then turn north on Route Phoenix. By driving up Phoenix from that side, they could hit the flank of the Muj that were attacking us. But the Muj deserve some credit, they planned their assault well. As the squad came down Michigan, they ran straight into an ambush that had been set for them. The Muj were in positions in buildings along the road. The side mirror of the lead vehicle was shot off, and the squad quickly turned around to come to our support via a different direction. In actuality, the grunt squad was likely the Muj's primary target while we were just the diversion used to draw them into the ambush. They attacked us just long enough, while disengaging in time to get away before they were in any serious danger. They knew where our support would be coming from and had ambushes well positioned for both us and our support. We didn't take any casualties and I don't think they did either, or at least not any killed. But had they of been more aggressive, we might have been in serious trouble.

We searched the ambush area and found an RPG launcher, an unfired RPG, a belt of RPK ammo, a grenade, an AK-47 with a round jammed in the chamber, and a couple of ammo magazines taped together for quick reload. I'm not sure why they dropped so many of their weapons unless they were starting to panic, or just wanted to get back into the city without weapons so they could quickly blend in with the civilians. We also found a black hood with eyeholes cut out, like the ones that the Al-Qaeda guys wore in the Nick Berg video. The hood smelled strongly of the guy's cologne or aftershave and looks like it was the corner of a black velvet pillowcase that was cut off with, for some reason, a dryer sheet sewn above the eyeholes. We also picked up a red and white Hajji scarf, which is worn by nearly everyone around here. I kept both, but told Hayne that he could have the scarf. I should really give it to Sherman or GG since they were next to me during the attack, or to Parrott since he killed the car bomber.

Shortly after we finished searching the area a LAV arrived, which ensured that the Muj wouldn't poke their heads out again. Around the same time, a large group of military-age males came pouring out of a building near the Phoenix/Michigan intersection and hopped into cars that had pulled up. I'm sure that they must have been the shooters that ambushed the infantry squad coming to support us. We yelled to the Captain but the cars raced off into the city and, in any event, we didn't have enough guys to go straight in after them. In talking to the Marine that was in the turret of the Captain's vehicle during the ambush, he said he saw the Hajji with the black hood during the ambush and had fired on him, hitting the rock he was hiding behind. He also said he was ordered not to fire the .50 cal. as the Captain was afraid that most of the shots would go over the insurgents and land in the city.

We stayed in the Triangle until dark before moving to set up an OP next to the power station on Route Michigan, west of the city. We could hear the nearest mosque's loudspeakers making announcements and the Muj celebratory shooting early in the night. We also saw the occasional green flare being fired into the sky, which we've been told by Goat Man is a call to arms. A helicopter that circled the area reported a large crowd of military age men gathered outside the western-most mosque, not far from the area of the Triangle. For some strange reason, it pisses me off to know that the Muj think they've won, or have in some way beaten us or scared us off. They obviously planned the ambush to last for a limited amount of time, but I wish it had lasted

117

just a little longer. In any case, I'm pretty happy with how I reacted. Once I finally figured out where the fire was coming from, I did what I was supposed to do. That question has always weighed on my mind and is impossible to answer until you've been put to the test. Reacting to an ambush is a little different than an IED or VBIED. The only down side was that at one point while rushing forward, I jumped into the small trench that we've been shitting in—at the time I couldn't have cared less.

Camp Korean Village, Iraq
November 20, 2004

Apparently the other team was hit on their last rotation as well but, luckily, none of our engineers were there. It happened in the same exact place, at nearly the same exact time of day. It sounds like the Hajjis were feeling a little braver after attacking us, they stuck around longer and fired five RPGs while keeping up sustained small-arms fire. Fortunately no one on our side was hit. I'm still trying to get the full story and, while there was obviously an ambush, I'm still not sure about some of the details. The grunt that I first spoke with in the chow hall has a big mouth, and I'm not sure I believe much of what he told me. The suspicious part of his story was when he said that the Muj sent a car bomb down Route Phoenix in the direction of the Triangle, but that our guys were able to kill the driver before he got close. Apparently, the car had a 2 × 4 board propped against the gas pedal so that it would keep going even if the driver was killed. It didn't work and the car ended up rolling off the side of the road, where it was eventually recovered by the insurgents. The whole story sounded strange and struck me a potential bullshit. I don't think our guys would have been pushed back to the point where the insurgents would risk trying to recover the car bomb. But if it was a car bomb, I'm not sure how we would know about the 2 × 4. If our guys were close enough to look inside, then how were the Muj able to recover it? What's more likely is that it was a civilian car that saw the ambush under way, swerved off the road after our guys fired on it, and then turned around to get out of there as quickly as possible. To be honest, everyone that I've talked to has a different version of events, so it's difficult to understand what really happened. It's bizarre, in less than forty-eight hours there's already embellishment. However, one thing is clear—our AO has now escalated from mortars, car bombings, and IEDs to serious, well-organized ambushes.

Also like us, one of the other team's positions received some pot-shots the day prior to the ambush. Unlike us, they went straight into the city to try and get the guy, searching a nearby house without finding anything. As they were leaving, they started taking more fire but weren't able to determine where it was coming from. That was the thing that struck me the most after we were ambushed. Try as I might, it was impossible to tell the direction of fire until I saw the RPG. Getting fired on from an unknown location was the most helpless, frustrating feeling. The infantry company commander had been with the other team on this last rotation. Apparently, he and the LAR company commander have now agreed to keep LAR primarily on the west side of town, which is where the most dangerous OPs are located. It will serve to distance us from the majority of action, which probably makes the most sense as LAVs have more firepower and better optics.

I was a little nervous going out on this last cycle after having been attacked on our last rotation, on top of hearing about the other team being hit. We were initially told that we would be setting up another vehicle checkpoint in the area of the Triangle in an effort to entice the insurgents out again. The plan had been to stage LAR somewhere out of view, so that they could rush in as soon as we were attacked. In the end, for some reason, we didn't do it. Despite the recent agreement between the company commanders, we were one of the few infantry squads that stayed on the west side for the majority of the rotation. It ended up being fairly quiet with no gunfire in the city, even at night. The last night of the rotation I went with the HET guy, Thomas the translator, and the Captain to talk to the Goat Man. He said that he hasn't heard much and since he hasn't seen us in a while, he doesn't ask around for news as often. He told us he works as a laborer, heading into town each day to try to find work—sometimes he does, sometimes he doesn't. But if we want him to get info for us on a regular basis, then we need to pay him a standard wage. I think he has proven himself to the point where he deserves a steady wage but the rules just don't allow it. The only bit of info he had, was that the guys we have been fighting are from Fallujah and he estimates that there are roughly a thousand of them in town. Something was either lost in translation or he is hugely exaggerating. While we know that a lot of people have fled to Ar Rutbah from Fallujah, there's no way that many fighters are in town. It's possible that he meant there are a total of a thousand refugees, of which maybe forty or fifty could be actively fighting.

He also mentioned that the Muj planned to use a car bomb to hit a seven-ton truck full of Marines while the last team was conducting a mission in the city. Evidently, U.S. funds that had been transferred to the city for the payment of the police and Iraqi National Guard had been stolen. So we brought in more money, this time under Marine escort, to turn over to the bank. Goat Man's story was that during the transfer, some guy named Mohammed stopped the insurgents from sending out the car bomb by telling them that we would kill everyone in retaliation. Who says fear can't be a deterrent? He told the bomber, who was from Fallujah, to go back and fight in Fallujah and that they don't want that kind of trouble in Ar Rutbah. The Goat Man also told us that a Hajji, whose name sounds like "Soccer," is the big shot in town and that he boasts about attacking us. It's all interesting, but not particularly helpful and may not even be true. I enjoy listening in on these interviews with the Goat Man. Most of the guys stay with the vehicles which we usually park a few hundred yards away in a wadi. The only reason I occasionally get to listen is because I volunteer to carry the radio. He's brought us some good info in the past but everything recent seems to increasingly be based on rumors or town gossip.

After we got back from the rotation we were told that as a result of the increase in hostilities, we were being elevated to Block Three. This is the first that I've heard of the "blocks," and have no idea what block we were on before. We were told that Block One means being nice and kissing babies, Block Two is a little more aggressive, and Block Three is considered open hostilities. So if they fire on us from a building, we can now light up the building. And next time we're ambushed, we can actually use the .50 cal., which would have ripped right through the shit they were hiding behind during the ambush. We were also told that we will start doing four-day cycles outside the wire instead of three. We've already done some of these, though I don't know what necessitated the change. We're all pretty exhausted by the end of a two or three-day rotation. I'm not sure I see the benefit of staying out longer, but it must somehow make things easier for the higher-ups. Like anything, it may be painful at first but once we get used to it, it'll soon become the norm.

Camp Korean Village, Iraq
November 27, 2004

We're back from another four-day rotation. It was absolutely miserable, primarily because of the dropping temperatures. It was cold as hell, getting down to twenty degrees one night. Normally that would be fine—twenty degrees isn't really that cold—but most of us don't have much cold weather gear. It's not too terrible during the day, when we are kept busy. But at night, especially while standing on watch, it gets old *real* fast. There was also a massive sand storm. I've been in a couple already, but nothing even close to this. We couldn't see ten feet in front of us as the whole world seemed to turn a brownish red. On the other team's previous rotation, a roving patrol had been hit by an IED on the intersection of Ski and Michigan. Apparently the intersection was under direct observation at all times with the exception of the storm, so they assume that that's when it was placed. When the sandstorm rolled in, we just happened to be set up on an OP near the same intersection. Parrott and I suggested that we take a small team close, in case they try to place an IED again. So Parrott, Sherman, and myself made our way over to it, and got set up in a ditch close enough to be able to see it through the storm. The position was perfect. While we could see the intersection, we were still far enough away that the Muj wouldn't have been able to see us if coming from the direction of the city. Unfortunately, they didn't try it this time—it would have been great if they did. Parrott had the SAW and I had an M203; we were just praying that a car would pull up.

Thanksgiving was OK. It's a day for family, so in this place it felt just like any other day. When we got back from the field, the chow hall had a nice meal set up for us—which was great. To be honest, I hadn't thought about Thanksgiving until it was nearly upon us. It's not as big a deal as Christmas and always has a way of sneaking up on me. Shortly after sitting down for our big meal, KV received some incoming mortars. A bunch of people jumped up and ran out of the chow hall to go out on react but since no one called for us, we stayed put and were able to avoid going. I didn't even stop eating. Speaking of, although not the most fearsome nickname, people have started calling me "chow monster" because I eat so much. The food around here can be hit or miss. The one meal from the chow hall on KV that I would happily eat back home, is the beef tips in BBQ sauce. In the field I opt for the beef enchilada or spaghetti MREs. With some hot sauce and jalapeno cheese, both are actually quite good.

Camp Korean Village, Iraq
December 1, 2004

I'm getting ready to go out for a four-day rotation. It's starting to get really cold at night, routinely getting down into the teens or low-twenties. It's not horrible, except that the wind kicks up as the sun goes down, which makes it feel much colder. When I'm in my sleeping bag it isn't bad, but standing in the turret for night watch can be miserable. The worst is when we go on patrol and are riding in the back of the Humvee. Below freezing temps while riding down the road at fifty miles per hour gets pretty damn cold, pretty damn fast. The other day we went on a raid and after the half hour drive to the city, everyone's hands and feet were so numb that it was hard to run towards the buildings. My legs felt like dead weight. When we jumped out of the back of the Humvee, everyone stumbled around like we were drunk. I was carrying the sledgehammer, and had the job of knocking in the door. Each hit felt like my hands were going to shatter. The grunts' Master Sergeant rode in the back of the high-back with us. Until then, I don't think any of the higher-ups had any idea of just how cold it has gotten. Afterwards, he said he would look into getting us some cold-weather gear. Before we left for California, our engineer battalion's Sergeant Major had told us not to bring any of our cold-weather stuff because we wouldn't need it. Sherman keeps repeating that if we ever see him again, he's going to tell him that he was full of shit.

It was all for nothing, as the raid ended up being a bust. The target was a nice house, with a couple of warehouses in back that were packed with cigarettes. The higher-ups must have been fairly confident that something, or someone, would be there. They even had us break out the mine detectors to search the grounds for a weapons cache but nothing turned up.

Camp Korean Village, Iraq
December 8, 2004

If I wasn't before, then it's now official: I'm tired of this place. Any excitement at being deployed or of seeing action is now completely gone. The temperature dropped to fifteen degrees the other night with a cold wind blasting us the entire time. In order to block the wind, we've started digging ditches to sleep in. I'm also starting to miss home, particularly at this time of year. Williamsburg during Christmastime is one of my favorite places in the world. Bundling up and walking through the old town, the smell of the fires, spending time with family—I really enjoy it. That said, if given the choice, I wouldn't go home if I knew that I would have to come back. I can't imagine how guys in the Army do it—to go home for just one week in the middle of a tour. They pull longer tours, so I can understand the need for time off, but it would be surreal to go home only to come right back.

I went on an off-cycle raid the other day. We spent hours driving in the open desert, early in the morning, looking for the target house complex. It's a supposed waypoint in the middle of nowhere, used by the Muj as a place to lay low. We were huddled in the back of the Humvee with sleeping bags draped over us in order to try and keep as warm as possible. It was nearly a full moon and the desert floor seemed to be glowing as if reflecting the moonlight. While driving around, we came across a shepherd with his flock. The way everything was lit by the pale moonlight, it seemed almost otherworldly. It felt like we had stumbled upon a scene from 2,000 years ago. The shepherd was silently standing with his donkey and a flock of sheep, surrounded by nothing but open desert and a sky full of stars. Seeing a shepherd isn't an unusual sight, but at that hour, and at this time of year—it was like we had gone through a time warp and emerged into biblical times. He

A sleeping ditch, used to stay out of the cold wind during the night.

watched us as we drove by, and we just stared back at him. As rapidly as things seem to change in this world, it can be easy to lose sight of how much things really stay the same.

We were notified the other day that two Marines in our AO were killed. The way things have been escalating, we had all assumed that it would only be a matter of time. Instead of occurring in the city, it was a car bomb attack at one of the border crossings. Specifically Trebil, the Jordanian border crossing. We regularly run helo patrols up the stretch of Route Mobile from KV to the border crossings and have even done a few vehicle patrols, which can take a long time. Still, I've never had a chance to get a good look at the bases. The crossings are manned by guys from KV, with people taking turns by rotating in and out. Fortunately, we haven't had to do it yet as I've heard that the base, if you can call it that, is very exposed. Burdette said that the road basically runs through the middle of it. We were outside the wire at the time of the attack but Burdette and Johnson, who were still at KV, had to quickly fly to Trebil as part of the react force. He said it was a sobering scene. After they arrived, which was only a few hours after the attack, they could still smell the explosives in the air. The only open racks to sleep in were those made vacant by the guys that had been killed and wounded. Apparently this isn't the first time the border crossing has been targeted by a car bomb and it's nearly impossible to defend against, since it's the job of the guys manning the borders to inspect all vehicles coming into and out of the country. The bomber doesn't even need to figure out a way to get close, he can just get in line and drive right up. I'm not sure how this attack will change our pace of ops, or distribution of forces. There's the potential that we'll begin maintaining a larger contingent at the borders now, although I really hope to avoid going.

We'll be heading out later today. It's been cold and rainy the past couple days, so I hope it clears before we head out.

Camp Korean Village, Iraq
December 15, 2004

I've been lackadaisical in my writing, a week between entries is too long. One of the infantry squads was ambushed at the beginning of our last rotation, immediately following the changeover with the other team. They were driving on the west side of the city, south on Route Phoenix towards Michigan, when they started taking fire from the direction of the city. Evidently, it took a while for the grunts to figure out where the fire was coming from. They eventually determined that it was originating in the area near the western-most mosque but before they could move in that direction, an IED went off. No one was hit, although the squad leader spilt hot coffee all over himself—everyone assumed his yelling and cursing on the radio was from being wounded. We were on the east side of the city at the time, so could only listen to updates and reports over the radio. It was bizarre to sit in the Humvee, listening to the play-by-play but unable to do anything to help. We heard the boom of the IED in the distance but couldn't hear any of the gunfire. While searching the area afterwards, the squad found a sand table model similar to ones that we use when planning an operation. It was a model of the immediate area, with little toy cars denoting the

125

grunts' patrol, and various firing positions and buildings marked. It's interesting to know that the insurgents do the exact same as us, in terms of planning, prior to an operation.

The only other hostile action on the rotation was related to the stories circulating about a professional-level sniper operating in the city. While no one has been hit yet, there have been a mounting number of pot shots made from long distances—distances that rule out the possibility of the shots being from a standard Muj with an AK. It may be a single guy taking the shots, or it may be a collection of random events that everyone assumes to be the work of a single sniper. The only instance that I've witnessed was the fire that we received on the southeast side of the city on the day preceding the ambush in the Triangle. Apparently the sniper, if that's what he is, took a shot at one of the infantry squads on our last rotation. Despite the fact that it was really windy for nearly the entire rotation, the sniper fired a long distance shot at a grunt that was leaning against a berm while manning an OP on the west side of the city. They estimated that the shot came from nearly one kilometer away and just barely missed hitting the grunt in the head. Hopefully the story has been exaggerated and the "sniper" is just a collection of unrelated events. No one likes the idea of a well-trained sniper running loose in the city.

In addition to the casualties at the border, we heard some sad news through the Charlie Company home network. Both of the other platoons in Charlie have been attached to other infantry battalions, similar to us. Third platoon is operating south of Baghdad, while first platoon is attached to the grunts that spearheaded the retaking of Fallujah. During the battle, some guys in first platoon were wounded and Brad Arms was killed. I didn't know him very well since he was in a different platoon. The majority of the time I had spent around him was during last summer's two-week training in Romania. He was a nice guy, a little younger than me. I remember joking with him while we were playing soccer against the Romanian soldiers. We've heard two different versions of how he was killed. One being that he was shot during an ambush while patrolling in Fallujah. The other is that he was hit by a sniper. We probably won't know the full story until we get home, if ever. Not that it's any consolation to his family, but I think either of those is better than an IED. We've reached the halfway point of the deployment I just hope we get through the second half without any more KIAs from the Company. I feel terrible for his family, particularly now that it's getting close to Christmas. I don't imagine that they'll ever be able to enjoy it again, at least not in the same way. Hopefully our families realize that Fallujah is totally different from where we are. Even so, losing one of our own is going to ratchet up everyone's anxiety.

Dad emailed a copy of an article that he found online about third platoon from Charlie Company—the platoon that has been stationed near Yusyfiyah, just south of Baghdad. Since we've had less news from the other platoons of Charlie than we've had from our own platoon, which hasn't been much, I decided to print it out in order to show the other guys. The article interviewed a couple of the guys from the platoon. It sounds like they have been doing similar stuff to us, although they seem more focused on searching for weapons caches. Aside from the first big weapons cache that we helped destroy, there haven't been too many in our AO. At most, we run across the occasional artillery shell or weapon. But even then, it's not typically in a big weapons cache that the insurgents have hidden. In fact, I would guess that most of the weapons we've found are just things that have been overlooked. What does that say about this country? It's not unusual for an artillery shell to be found lying randomly in the desert. Of course, that's not to say that there aren't more large caches in the area. With so many old Iraqi military bases around Ar Rutbah, I'm positive that there are many more. But without informants, locating a cache is nearly impossible.

I knew that first platoon had been sent to a hot AO, since they are in Fallujah. But it sounds like third platoon is in a busy area as well. The article mentioned that they have found RPGs, sniper rifles, machine guns, scopes, and all kinds of explosives for making IEDs or car bombs. The article stated that in a single cache, they found over nine hundred artillery rounds. With each IED containing two or three artillery rounds, that's the equivalent of getting four hundred IEDs out of insurgent hands. While we've come across most, if not all, of the same types of weapons—we're not doing it nearly as frequently, and definitely not in those kinds of quantities. Part of the reason may be that, at this point, we are essentially being used as grunts. And while they're definitely doing a worthwhile mission—arguably more important than ours—I'm happier doing the kinds of missions that we've been doing. I'd rather go on patrols and raids than search and sweep areas for weapons caches.

Camp Korean Village, Iraq
December 25, 2004

I got back from outside the wire this morning and figure I should write a couple lines since its Christmas. We're supposed to get a big meal tonight, which will be nice. The power in our tent has stayed on all day—a Christmas miracle. I thought that perhaps Christmas would make me feel homesick but it really hasn't had too much of an effect. In fact, until today, I really haven't thought much about it. It probably has to do with the fact that it doesn't feel very Christmassy around here. If I were anywhere else in the world then I'd probably feel more homesick. But we're into a routine now and Christmas feels like any other day. I'm sure it's not going to be a very enjoyable Christmas for the family, but it's all downhill from here.

This last rotation wasn't too bad: we had an RPG fired at us, an IED explode in front of us, and heard a friendly fire incident—although listing everything makes it sound much more exciting than it really was. At the start, we were linked with one of the infantry squads and conducted some routine OPs, vehicle checkpoints, and roving patrols. We did one short foot-patrol along the outskirts of the city where we made our way up Michigan and into the city, before turning back towards Phoenix. Early on one of the evenings, while at an OP on the north side of Mobile, we heard what sounded like an explosion. Everyone hung around the radio, waiting to hear what had happened. From the radio chatter, we were able to piece together that one of the infantry squads had accidentally fired on one of the LAR patrols. As it turns out, the LAR patrol was rolling up behind an infantry roving patrol. In the dark, the grunt in the turret couldn't see what was approaching, and went through the process of waving his arms and signaling with a flashlight. LAR kept coming, rapidly gaining on the infantry Humvees, so the grunt fired a shot from the 50 cal. to warn them off—realizing too late that he was firing on our own guys. We didn't find out these details until we got back to KV, but could piece together what had happened. As it turned out, one of the LAR guys took a bit of shrapnel in his face as the 50 cal. round pierced the LAV. Otherwise, everyone was OK—but it was a scare for the LAR guys. As LAR raced down Mobile to evacuate the wounded, their platoon commander radioed in something to the effect of "we're coming down Mobile, try not to shoot us." From that, we could assume at what had happened but didn't yet know if the situation was serious. It's crazy, in the dead of night the grunt's 50 cal., even from a mile away, sounded as loud as an IED going off.

Later in the rotation, I was separated from GG, Parrott, Hayne, and Sherman. LAR was conducting a raid/patrol in the city without infantry—which was a first—and, for whatever reason, wanted an engineer to go with them. I grabbed everything I had in terms of explosives and loaded my assault pack, then squeezed into the back of one of their LAVs. Those things definitely aren't built for guys my size. I had my knees nearly jammed into my chest and couldn't wait to get out. We were dropped off at what looked like a row of storage units in the southern section of the city. One of the LAR officers asked if I had enough explosives to blow off all the locks so that they could search them. I told him that I could, but was never asked to do it. We then patrolled deeper into the city, with the front of the patrol stopping to search through a building while we waited along the road. After fifteen minutes, an RPG was fired in our direction. The Muj had fired it and then immediately fled. I didn't see them and it didn't hit too close to anyone. But it's actions like that which make it feel like we're fighting against ghosts. They fire a shot, set off an IED, or fire an RPG—and we never even catch a glimpse of them. The atmosphere was tense for a couple minutes but after it became clear that it wasn't the start of an ambush, we shrugged it off and went back to patrolling.

Once back with my team, we moved to the west side of the city. On the last day, yesterday, we were doing a roving patrol—driving up and down the Triangle. We would drive east on Michigan, then turned north on Phoenix, then southwest on Ski. In the process, we unknowingly drove past an IED that was placed at the Route Michigan/Ski intersection at least three times, if not more. Even though we were all paying attention, it was impossible to see. Luckily for us, we had been driving southwest on Ski. By approaching the intersection from that

Marines on a foot patrol in Ar Rutbah, Iraq.

direction, the bombed-out hospital and some other buildings obstructed the Muj's view. As far as I can tell, that's the only reason that they didn't set it off on us. As we patrolled, there was squad of grunts at an OP at the base of the Triangle and after our last loop, we pulled into their position in order to trade places. We manned the OP, while they went on a roving patrol. As they started driving north on Ski, the IED blew up. They had approached the intersection in the opposite direction from us and were therefore under observation from the triggerman in the city the entire time. Fortunately as it turned out, the way in which the IED had been placed meant that the blast was directed away from them and back towards us. We heard shrapnel fly by overhead, which sounded like a sheet of metal being flapped around. No one was hurt, although some of the grunts in the rover patrol were stunned. We were all surprised, I can't believe we drove by it so many times without ever noticing. One of the grunts happened to be taking a picture of the squad as they approached the intersection, right as the IED went off. Immediately after the blast, we all jumped back into the vehicles. It felt

130

like we should respond in some way, either by racing into the city or doing something else. The problem was, with the entire west side of the city facing us, we had no idea where to go or what we could do. We ended up just staying at the OP, but it left me with an eerie feeling—to know that we were being watched by the Muj the entire time. Just knowing that someone was watching our movements with the intention of killing us, while we unknowingly drove around scanning the area while talking. It just reinforces that sense that we're fighting ghosts.

That's perhaps the most unsettling thing about any kind of action in this place. As I look over what I've written, it almost sounds like a real war—with RPGs being fired at us and IEDs going off in front of us. I did the math and the reality is that it was just a few brief minutes of excitement from a total of over 5,700 minutes of the rotation. The other 5,695 minutes were boring and monotonous. Thankfully, no one was hurt by the IED attack, but it could have easily turned out differently if they had placed it correctly. Their timing was good, so the blast should have hit the grunts' vehicle square on—sending shrapnel ripping through their high-back and into the Marines sitting there. Instead of a few brief moments of excitement in an otherwise boring rotation, it could have turned into a truly tragic day, made all the worse by the fact that we weren't doing a mission of any consequence. We were just rolling around the edge of the city for no real reason in particular.

Camp Korean Village, Iraq
December 31, 2004

It's already New Year's Eve—time flies. I hadn't even realized it until I wrote the date at the top of the page. Someone just told me that we're each to be given a can of beer to celebrate but we're only allowed to drink it under supervision in the chow hall—should be a wild time. The cold weather has made rotations outside the wire more and more miserable, although I was finally able to draw some cold weather gear from supply, which has helped. I've also received some new books from home, including one on the history of the First Crusade. We're east of where those events occurred but just being in an Arab, desert landscape makes it easier to imagine. When chatting with the HET guy on KV, I looked through some of the translated insurgent propaganda. Most of the propaganda doesn't even refer to us as Americans, instead it calls us Crusaders. It's almost laughable, but reminded me that these people see the world in a very different way than us. Most Americans don't know the first thing about the Crusades and before reading this book, I only knew the little that I'd seen in a couple documentaries. Yet to these people, the Crusades are something that still resonates within their collective memory. The propaganda also made some other outrageous claims, like that we hang crosses from the barrels of our tanks. The Muj know their audience, so that bullshit must work, but it's hard to believe that the people take it seriously. One would think that the average Iraqi has seen enough of us to know that we aren't trying to forcibly convert them, or otherwise subjugate them. We're not demanding tribute, nor are we actively repressing them or their religion. We're just trying to keep things as safe and stable as possible, so that we can get the hell out of here. While we may not necessarily do it in the kindest, gentlest way—it must be better than when Saddam was running the show. But I suppose if you've been force-fed propaganda for your entire life, both by Saddam and now the Muj, then you likely have a skewed worldview.

Things on KV have gotten much more comfortable. We share the tent with some guys from the Trucks Company, and they've built a couch out of some pallets to make a living room area around the TV. Naseem, the translator, bought us a satellite dish when he went home for vacation. It cost $100 and looks a little funny as it's jerry-rigged to the top of our tent, but we can now watch TV. Most of the channels that we are able to get are from Europe, so we tend to just leave it on MTV to listen to the music. One of the Trucks guys even managed to scrounge up an Iraqi washing machine, which we've set up in the corner of the tent. It doesn't get clothes too clean, but it's better than doing them by hand. We dug a ditch next to the tent for the water to drain into but as soon as an officer sees it filled with stagnant water, we'll probably be ordered to get rid of the machine. Not that I can blame them, it's definitely not sanitary. But considering that half the guys piss out of the front tent flap during the night, instead of walking to the porta-potties, our tent isn't exactly sanitary to begin with. The rumor is that an Army unit may be arriving soon to install shower and laundry tents in the next few weeks.

When Naseem brought the satellite dish to our tent, we were all in shock—his face looked like one giant bruise. He's the least cautious of all of our translators, sometimes not even covering his face when talking to other Iraqis. While on vacation, he visited home and someone either recognized him or guessed at where he had been. He was taken hostage, held for three days, and severely beaten. He said that he expected to be killed but fortunately, he has a large family that is very well connected. A group of his sons was able to track him down and, with the help of some neighbors, rescued him. He said that he knew some of the people that had kidnapped him but he refused to tell the higher-ups. He seemed confident that his family can protect him and that getting us involved would only make things worse. Besides, he never broke down and admitted to being a translator for us which, after the beating the kidnappers put him through, they just might believe him—Naseem's a tough old guy. Our other translator, Thomas, is also an interesting guy. He's not an Iraqi but rather a Christian from the south of Sudan, and speaks seven languages. His dad was a doctor and his mom was a schoolteacher. He was separated from his family years ago in the violence and upheaval there, and eventually fled the country. He hasn't seen or heard from his family since but seems to speak under the assumption that they are still alive somewhere. He's been in Iraq since the invasion and, above all, has a visceral hatred of Muslims. He doesn't plan on leaving Iraq until the U.S. does, and will tell anyone that'll listen that we should invade Syria next. I can't help but pity him, without a family or country to return to, I'm not sure what the future has in store for him. We've mentioned that he should look into getting his U.S. citizenship. If anyone deserves it, it's Thomas.

As far as the field, it's been more of the same and we're still doing the four-day rotations. The biggest change is that some construction engineers arrived at KV to build a small base just outside of Ar Rutbah, off the side of Route Phoenix. We've been calling it the "JBCC" for Joint Border Crossing Center but since all the infantry guys are from Texas they, of course, call it Fort Texas. It's been set up around some gutted Iraqi buildings, on a hill about a half mile from the city. We had previously commandeered the area as a base while on rotations but now it's been formalized as a U.S. base. The construction engineers built a berm around it and put in some machine gun posts and barbed wire. Having the JBCC does make things much easier for the team that's outside the wire. We now have a place to operate from that isn't a half hour drive from the city. I'm sure the insurgents aren't thrilled. Not that it's changed the way we operate in any way, but now there is a small U.S. base set right along the main road into the city. It projects a degree of control over the city, which in the battle for hearts and minds must have some kind of impact.

While on the last rotation we were sitting in the radio room of the JBCC listening to the LAR guys over the radio, when they were hit by an IED. They were on patrol, moving towards the city from the south on Route Mercury. As they approached the city the IED went off, injuring one of the LAR guys. The LAVs wheeled into line facing the city, but couldn't identify any targets to engage. That's the main frustration that everyone has. I've said it before, but it's like we're fighting ghosts.

An LAV standing guard over the desert west of Ar Rutbah, from an overlook position in the Joint Border Crossing Center.

134

We almost never see them and even if we do, they're gone before we can do anything. The wounded LAR guy was raced to the JBCC, where we watched as he was loaded into a Black Hawk medical helicopter for transport back to KV. He could walk on his own, and didn't seem too badly hurt.

We've started doing daily patrols into the city. I'm not sure what the purpose is, other than to try and focus the Muj's attention on us rather than on Mobile. If anything, it probably makes things easier for them. If their objective is to simply inflict as many casualties as possible, then that's much easier to accomplish from inside the city, rather than venturing out onto the roads that we regularly patrol. In the city, we only control whichever streets we happen to be standing on at any given time. As soon as we round the corner and are out of sight, the street is back in their control.

I imagine things will be hectic once I get home, which we've been told could be as early as mid–April. I'll have about three months until college starts, a month of which I'd like to spend traveling to visit family and friends. It's going to be weird to go back to school. I wasn't that good with girls to begin with, a year of sitting around the desert with a bunch of Marines isn't going to help. Come to think of it, I haven't seen a real woman in a long time. There are only a couple on base and we don't see very many in the city. Even when we do, they're usually running inside. I'm still not sure what I'll do after school. There's a good chance that I may be sent back to this place again, which makes it hard to get excited about anything.

We heard that there was a massive tsunami that hit Asia. I'm not sure yet what the real story is, it'll probably take some time before the press sorts out fact from fiction.

Camp Korean Village, Iraq
January 9, 2005

While we were outside the wire on the last rotation, some of the grunts from the other team were finally able to capture one of the Muj that has been mortaring KV. From the sound of it, it was more of a fluke than anything. A squad was on a routine patrol around the perimeter of KV and came across some rockets rigged with a timer to fire on the base. As far as I know, the insurgents haven't launched rockets at KV before, it's always been mortars. The only rocket attack I've seen was the one at Al Asad—which seems so long ago now. Allegedly, the patrol stopped the timer with only five minutes left before the rockets were to launch. They then raided the nearest house and the guy living there confessed to mortaring the base. They also found some weapons and ammo. As far as I know, that's the only guy we've nabbed thus far, although there must have been more than one. As much as the Abu Ghraib incident may have hurt our efforts in this country, it does have the benefit of making the insurgents absolutely terrified of being shipped to one of the detainment centers—so there's a good chance he'll squeal on his friends.

We heard some bad news from our engineer platoon. Since leaving them, they've continued to run missions out of Al Asad. But at some point, they were moved from there to Haditha Dam—an area just north of Al Asad and closer to some of the cities and towns along the Euphrates River. They are still all together, supporting the various infantry units in their AO, so we are the only squad that ended up being separated. While doing a mission out of Haditha Dam, our platoon commander, Captain Kuniholm, was seriously wounded in an ambush. We haven't heard from our platoon very often and don't yet know the full story, but the rumor that has circulated is that he was on a boat patrol on the Euphrates. They had disembarked after taking fire from the riverbank and, after patrolling inland for a bit, were ambushed and he was severely wounded from either an IED, mortar, or RPG. There are obviously still a lot of unknowns and the only fact that we do know, is that he wasn't shot. Instead, it was some kind of indirect fire or RPG. The wound is severe and he has lost his arm. It was terrible to hear, but we're all thankful that it wasn't more serious. Like most Marine officers, he seems to be a motivated guy, so I'm sure he won't let it hold him back—Marine officers are a different breed. Shortly after hearing about Captain Kuniholm, we each received a box of Christmas gifts from his family. All very useful stuff, which had the effect of making us feel even worse about what had happened. I'm sure this will be hard on his family, but at least he's alive and will be safe at home.

Hayne, our driver, isn't going out on anymore rotations since he's now permanently working in the repair and maintenance shop. Apparently we aren't going to get a new driver, so have been taking turns driving. Last rotation, I drove a couple nights and nearly killed us on two occasions. We were on the east side of the city, watching the lights of a long convoy making its way east on Mobile, when we saw some sparks and heard the boom of mortars being fired. The mortar men appeared to be on the edge of the east side, no further than a mile from us. We quickly loaded up and raced through the dark desert to get to them and in the rush, I nearly drove into a huge crater. By the time I saw it, it was nearly too late. I slammed on the brakes and we skidded to a stop right at the edge of the drop off. The lights haven't been working on our Humvee, which isn't normally an issue since we drive in blackout, but in this case they would have *really* come in handy. It's difficult to drive quickly through the desert with nothing but NVGs, especially if there's no ambient light. We didn't get to the mortar men in time. In fact, I think they were likely further away than it initially appeared. While returning to our OP, I led the way in the Humvee as a seven-ton truck full of grunts followed us. I ended up driving through a gap between a transmission tower and a power line going to the ground. I hadn't noticed it, and the Humvee fit right through the gap. But the seven-ton couldn't fit, and smacked into the powerline. It sent sparks everywhere and knocked out the power to Germantown. Whoops. The guys in the seven-ton accused me of trying to kill them.

The next day of that rotation, one of the infantry squads ran over a landmine which had been planted next to Germantown but, fortunately for them, it didn't go off. Germantown sits on a hill, so it's a good spot to set up an OP and observe the area and the mine was buried in some gravel at one of these often-used OPs. We use this particular OP a lot as it gives an unimpeded view of a long stretch of Route Michigan, including a section that the unit we replaced called "IED Alley," although we've only had one or two IEDs there. Also, the OP is very well concealed, being covered by a large shed on one side and a berm on the other. We should obviously be mixing up the use of our OPs more frequently, the insurgents are clearly taking note. GG and I were called to destroy the mine. It was a very new-looking, tan colored Italian mine—similar to one we found the other day on the west side of the city. I remember Sergeant Moose's landmine identification class from San Mateo, when he said "Ruffles have ridges, and Italians do too." It makes absolutely no sense, but is catchy enough that I'll always remember that Italian mines have ridges. The mine on the west side of the city had been placed on top of the ground along a dirt track, just south of Michigan. But this one was much better placed and had been well covered with gravel. Considering that the grunts drove right over the top of it, it must not have been set up correctly.

After arriving, we swept the area with the mine detectors to make sure it was clear and blew up the mine in place. Prior to blowing it, the Captain called some of the villagers from Germantown to come over and take a look. He tried to emphasis the danger that the Muj exposed their children to, by placing a landmine so near their village. In truth, it was probably someone in the village that placed the mine. After getting back to KV, I saw a pamphlet that was put together by some of the public relations guys. It showed a picture of the mine and said stuff in Arabic, assumedly about the dangers posed by the Muj. It was slightly comical, the picture clearly showed Humvee tire tracks in the gravel going right over top of the mine.

We also did a short foot patrol through Lukenbok, the only village where the people seem somewhat friendly. It's always fun to patrol that area, the kids pester us but don't throw rocks. It's hard not to feel sorry for them. It's probably the poorest village in the area and yet they still come out to bring us tea and sweets. We ended up giving them our box of MRE leftovers, which is made up of all the stuff we don't want to eat, but I'm sure they loved it.

Camp Korean Village, Iraq
January 10, 2005

Dad emailed a short article that mentioned KV. I'm surprised that anything from this area makes it into the press back home. The article was essentially a roundup of detainees taken in various parts of Iraq in recent days, and mentioned the Muj that had been caught with the rockets prepped to fire on KV. Mom and Dad must be on the computer all the time, looking for news of us. I'd rather they didn't see stuff like this since I try to tell them that we're in a city that's generally friendly towards us. And while it's quieter than a lot of places in Iraq, it's still not completely safe and I don't want them worrying more than necessary. Articles like this make it sound worse than it is. They now probably picture a base that's under constant fire. And while we receive a decent amount of mortar fire, it's pretty harmless. I can't wait to get home, if only for their sakes. The article stated that a group of Muj had been observed setting up the rockets to fire at the base, which was news to me. I didn't realize that a group had been observed. I'd heard that our guys just happened to stumble onto the rockets and then searched the nearest house—which is probably closer to the truth.

Outside Ar Rutbah, Iraq
January 14, 2005

I decided to bring my journal with me outside the wire, so figure I should write a line or two since it's almost my birthday. I'm on break at an OP overlooking Mobile. I've always used my birthday as an opportunity to plan what I want to accomplish in the year. I've tried thinking it over for this coming year, but I'm not sure where to even start. It's probably more important than ever, since in a year's time I'll have started my last semester at school. I should really figure out what I want to do with my life but the way units have been rotating in and out of Iraq and Afghanistan, I think we'll probably be coming back by late-2006—which puts a damper on any potential, long-term plans.

It may be wishful thinking, but it seems to be getting a little warmer. It still gets down into the twenties at night but the wind isn't as strong and the days seem a little warmer. Either that, or I'm just getting used to the cold.

Camp Korean Village, Iraq
January 18, 2005

The guys at school sent me some Crown Royal, which they had hidden by pouring it into a big Listerine bottle. I planned to save it, but that idea didn't last long. We ended up drinking it all last night with the guys from the Trucks Company. Towards the end of the night, I almost made the mistake of walking over to the phone center to call home. Fortunately, GG convinced me that it would be a bad idea. I'm glad he did. If caught, I would have been in serious trouble. Aside from the one beer that we've been given, I haven't had a drink since the last night before shipping to Iraq. It definitely caught up with me later that night, and I ended up puking into an empty Pringles can next to my rack. I completely forgot about it until today when I grabbed the can to eat some Pringles with lunch. It made for a really rough day but was probably the most fun we've all had in a long while.

Dad sent me a printout of a BBC article in his last letter. It gives a pretty grim view of the last year in Iraq, as well as of the future of this godforsaken place. It almost seemed like the article's author was reveling in the fact that things aren't going well, it had an "I told you so" tone running through the entire piece. But even the people that were protesting the war can't be happy to see the country descending into chaos, with both Iraqis and Americans being killed every day. The article went through a litany of the standard topics: Abu Ghraib, the post-invasion security vacuum, Coalition underestimation of the insurgency, bad planning, and failed policies. It did emphasize the importance of the upcoming elections, right before it dismissed them as not likely to work. No one has talked much about the elections around here and I didn't even know until recently that it would be happening so soon. I'm not sure what we'll be doing in terms of preparation for our AO, but I assume we'll be protecting voters and polling stations. It'll either be just another, boring day or will be a complete shit show—I'm guessing it'll be the former.

Articles like this always provide a jolting reminder that this place, as remote and distant as it feels to those of us that are here, is under the scrutiny of the entire world. Analysts in governments and think tanks the world over spend countless hours trying to figure out what will happen. People from London to Tokyo read about Iraq on a daily basis. It didn't really strike me as odd until I got here. It's strange to think that the cities of this country, most of which the people back home have never heard of, should command so much attention from around the world. The news back home—every article, news channel, or politician's speech—seems to be cloaked in geopolitical maneuvering. There's always some kind of angle behind the way Iraq is reported, you never get the unadulterated truth. But when you're actually here, it's all so simple. The ground truth is that every day some poor, uneducated young guys with AKs are chasing, and being chased by, young guys with M16s. That's about as simple as it gets. It almost seems like the events occurring in the Iraq featured on the nightly news are actually taking place in some other country.

JBCC (outside city of Ar Rutbah), Iraq
January 27, 2005

I haven't written in a while, so I'll try to relate everything in order of how it happened. It's been a terrible few days.

Our last rotation wasn't too bad. The JBCC was mortared on both the second and third days, which has become routine since the Muj can safely fire at us from inside the city. In one of the machine gun positions, guys have started writing the number of mortar rounds per day on the plywood roof. During one of the mortar attacks, we were manning an OP on the far side of Mobile. It was interesting to sit and watch as the mortars hit around the base—a total of nine in all. On the second day, we got a call that a kid had approached an LAR OP on the northwest side of the city. The kid was trying to talk to the LAR guys, so we were called in to bring Naseem over to translate. The kid's story was bizarre. He wanted to turn his dad in to us because, that morning, they had gotten into a big argument. The argument apparently ended with his father handing him an AK, and telling him to go shoot at the LAR OP. The kid knew that he'd be killed, so he stashed the gun and turned himself in. This wasn't a typical father-son tiff. His dad evidently didn't care that he was sending his son to die. The kid told us that his dad smuggled RPGs and other weapons into Fallujah prior to the operation to retake the city. He also said that he'd tell us where his uncle's been hiding, who is apparently on our wanted list. On top of that, he told us that he has seen the guys that have been mortaring the JBCC, saying that they fire from a wadi on the west side of town. He said that they drive a white Nissan pickup truck, which matches descriptions that we've heard before. They wear masks, but he could tell that one

141

of them is a guy with the last name of Palastini or Falastini, something like that. I recognized the name as one of the guys we've tried to nab on previous raids. Apparently we took his innocent brother while raiding a house recently but haven't caught up to him yet. He seems to be the main young thug in Ar Rutbah. It's hard to know how much of the kid's story is true, he was pretty upset. I've learned that in this place, people will tell us whatever they think we want to hear. I asked Naseem what he thought about the kid and he just seemed to pity him, saying that he had a messed up family life. He said the kid wanted to be arrested because he just didn't want to go home. It almost feels like we're the Stasi or Gestapo or something, with kids ratting on their own parents. We took him to the JBCC so that the HET guy could talk to him. If his father really is running weapons, then maybe something good can come of this.

Since getting back to KV, we heard that the other team reacted to some shooting in town by racing down into the city to investigate. Some Muj had been attempting to steal a truckload of cars and the Iraqi National Guard actually turned out to fight them. It's good to hear that they're attempting to maintain some degree of civil order. After the mayor's house was set on fire a few weeks ago, we all assumed that there is no real government or authority left in the city. Although I'm not sure that the ING would lift a finger if the insurgents were attacking us, at least they are doing something of value. As the other team arrived at the scene, they opened fire on who they thought to be the insurgents. It turned out to be ING guys that weren't in uniform. The grunts accidentally killed one and wounded a couple others, including the ING Captain. After being wounded, the ING Captain was more pissed at the Muj than us and told the grunts the names of the Muj that have been firing mortars at the JBCC. That's the story I've heard anyway, we'll see if anything comes of it.

On our second night off in KV, we were told that we would be doing a raid on a truck stop a long way east on Mobile. It ended up taking all night. We had reporters and a camera crew from ABC in the seven-ton truck with us, who were doing a piece on the borders. The ride took forever and was absolutely freezing. We were looking for Palastini or Falastini, the supposed insurgent ringleader in our area. Evidently we had good intel from three different sources, all of which told us that he has been staying at this truck stop. We were also told, for whatever reason, to expect to find him hiding in the rafters—which sounded strange. As per usual, the raid was a bust and we didn't find anything. All we ended up doing was interrupting the sleep of the old men who run the truck stop. I felt bad, as I was guarding them they kept trying to tell me something but we just couldn't get over the language barrier. They were getting frustrated and I had given up even attempting to decipher what they were saying. It finally dawned on me that they wanted to refill their power generator before it died. I spent a large part of the raid guarding the old men and chatting with the ABC cameraman. He is from New Zealand and lives in London. It would be cool to travel all over the world, seeing events that are considered newsworthy—an adventurous life.

The next day we heard about the worst military disaster to date in either Iraq or Afghanistan. A helicopter that was carrying most of a platoon of Marines from 1/3 crashed outside of Ar Rutbah due to mechanical issues. Thirty-one Marines were killed—almost the entire platoon, except for the eight or so guys that were in the other bird. It was the single deadliest day for U.S. troops in Iraq. Some of the guys from the Trucks Company in our tent drove their seven-ton trucks to the crash site, in order to help guard it and pick up debris. Evidently, the platoon that crashed had only a couple weeks left before they were to leave Iraq. They were coming from Fallujah, after having been part of the attack on the city and were supposed to help us with the elections. They were probably hoping to have a quiet couple weeks before finishing their tour and going home. I'm glad we didn't get called out to the crash site. I saw some pictures and wouldn't have wanted to see it in person. I helped sort through some of the mangled gear from the helicopter. Anything with a serial number had to be documented. All the rifles were melted and bent, it was an impossible task. Even though we obviously didn't know them, the entire base was in a somber mood after the news circulated. It's sad enough when one or two Marines have been killed, but to lose nearly an entire platoon is unbearable.

As if the day couldn't get any worse, in the afternoon we received some horrible news regarding our own platoon. When we'd heard about Captain Kuniholm being wounded, it had been relatively straightforward. We were notified by the grunts' CO that he had been injured, it was not a mortal wound, and that he would be on his way home as soon as possible. This time, we were simply told by one of the grunts' officers that "there had been a casualty" in our platoon and to standby for more info. We were told in the afternoon but didn't yet know who it was, or what the extent may be, until that evening. We were tense and nervous, hoping that it had only been a minor wound rather than someone being killed. It was an excruciating wait. I was walking to the officers' house for the fifth time to ask for an update when I saw Burdette walking out. I asked him if he knew any names yet, and he looked up with a blank look on his face and said in a deadpan voice, "let me see if I can remember them all." I felt like I'd been hit in the face, I still feel sick thinking about it now. I expected to hear about one guy getting hurt, maybe killed. Instead, our platoon had four killed and five wounded. I can't imagine a worse scenario, none of us expected something like this. Killed: Weaver, Bowling, Linn, and Strong. Wounded: Frances, Miller, Frederick, Meyers, and Gunnison. Almost a third of our platoon, dead or wounded.

The memorial service for the 30 Marines and Navy corpsman killed in the helicopter crash outside of Ar Rutbah on January 26, 2005.

144

When we didn't know who had been hit, I was still holding onto the hope that it had been an administrative mistake and that it wasn't actually anyone from our unit. I knew that we couldn't really be that lucky, but this is on the far end of the spectrum from what I had imagined possible. Burdette and I went back to the tent and told GG, letting him make the announcement. Some guys cried, I just continued to feel sick and stunned. For me personally, it was probably hardest to hear about Weaver and Strong; out of the four, I had been closest to them. Weaver and I were so very similar. Maybe it's because we were both into history, both tall, or because we come from military families—but I always felt close to him. I'd like to think the feeling was mutual. When we were in Vegas, he had me listen to some music by a Russian men's choir, saying that I would appreciate it. I think Burdette is in shock about Weaver. They both went to Virginia Tech and joined the unit around the same time.

Strong was just such a character and everyone liked him. He was funny and one of the most genuinely nice guys I've ever met. He was one of the few people I've met who could balance the fine line between being very religious and still being a lot of fun. I didn't know Bowling as well, he was a little quieter. He struck me as the kind of guy you'd want your daughter to bring home. He didn't complain and always seemed to do the right thing. I recall being on guard duty during my first AT at 29 Palms with him. He wouldn't let a group of Special Forces guys into the armory we were guarding because they didn't have their ID cards. Anyone else would have been awed by SF guys and would have just folded and let them in—especially when they started getting pissed. But Bowling wouldn't bend until they went back to get their IDs. In my mind, that epitomized his character. I didn't know Linn, apparently he had joined the platoon after we were already in country. At this point, all we can do is hope that the wounded aren't too serious. I'm guessing that since so many were killed, most of the wounded have more than just superficial wounds. I joined the unit only a little before Frances, while Meyers had taken me under his wing when I first joined. Miller is a nice, real quiet guy who was also with us in Vegas—I don't even think he's twenty-one yet. Frederick is a good guy too, still in school. I didn't know Gunnison very well, since he and his brother are volunteers from Delta Company in Tennessee, the same as Parrott.

They're all good guys, and we all wish we were with the rest of the platoon now. It would somehow be easier to take the news if we were with the other guys. We feel alone out here, most of the grunts have no idea what has happened to us.

We still only have limited information as to how it happened. Apparently, they were on their way back to base after a raid with LAR, when they were ambushed. We were told that they may have been the only high-back Humvee in the convoy, which would have made them the obvious, most vulnerable target. I'm not sure if everyone had been packed into one Humvee, or if they were spread into different vehicles. The after action report we were able to quickly look at, said that they were hit by an IED. But it also said that the attack included RPG, RPK and AK fire from a mosque, house, bridge and two alleyways—so at this point, it's impossible to know what happened. We're also not sure if anyone else in the convoy was hit, or if the only casualties were from our platoon. I'm still in shock about it all. The phone center has been closed because of the helo crash, which was particularly bad timing since we all desperately wanted to call our families to let them know that we are OK. Luckily, I was able to borrow a satellite phone from one of the Wolfpack contractors last night. Since it's unlikely that the names from either the helo crash, or our platoon's KIAs, have been reported to the families yet—I knew that Mom and Dad would be stressing. Ar Rutbah will likely be in the news because of the crash, if it isn't already. Then, once word gets out among the family network that there have been casualties in our unit, they would have naturally assumed the worse. I wasn't able to get a hold of anyone at home, but did leave a message. I told them that I'm OK, but won't be able to talk for a while since we would be going out for the elections. I'm so glad that I was able to get hold of that phone, I wouldn't want my parents to go through days of waiting, wondering if I'm alive.

With all the shit that happened yesterday, it reminds me that we're still a long ways from going home. We're getting close, but these elections will be dangerous for all of us. I'm in charge of the engineer team in the field this time, although it's only Parrott, Sherman and myself. GG has been sent to Walid, the border crossing with Syria, to help protect the polling station being set up there. Johnson was sent to Trebil, the crossing on the Jordanian border. Burdette went to the small town of Akashat, north of KV and Ar Rutbah. Wallace and Quinn are in the rear at KV and will come out in a couple days to replace us.

The rumor is that we'll be heading back to Al Asad on Feb 18, so only a few weeks to go.

Camp Korean Village, Iraq
February 10, 2005

I haven't written in nearly two weeks, so desperately need to catch up. The last time I wrote was on the twenty-seventh of January, the day after the helo crash and of learning about the casualties from our platoon. It was also the first day of a long rotation in which we were outside the wire in order to support the first Iraqi elections. Going into the rotation, everyone was a little nervous and unsure about what to expect. When changing over with the other team, I told Wallace the names of the casualties from our platoon. He had been at the JBCC at the time and only knew that we had taken casualties, but they couldn't relay the names to him over the radio. He looked just as stunned as we had been. All he said was "Jesus," then kept packing up his gear and walked away without saying another word.

I was in charge of our small fire-team for the rotation. Polling stations had been set up just outside of Ar Rutbah, in both border towns, and in the town of Akashat. Things were fairly quiet on the twenty-seventh and twenty-eighth. On the evening of the twenty-ninth, the day before the elections, we went with the XO (Executive Officer) from the LAR Company to check out a civilian vehicle which had been pulled over on the side of Mobile. When we arrived, it was apparent that the vehicle had been shot to hell by the Muj. We were told that the driver was a member of the Iraqi National Guard. When we first arrived at KV, there had been a fairly significant ING presence in the area—they even conducted occasional VCPs along Mobile. But sometime in October it was confirmed that they had abandoned their post, leaving the ING HQ completely deserted. The unit was eventually rebuilt but the Muj have never really bothered them. At worse, they view the ING as complacent and at best, as complicit. But recently some new ING guys have moved onto KV and have been mixed into the local unit. The local unit is primarily made up of guys from in and around Ar Rutbah, so the higher-ups made the change to ensure that the ING develop as a national force and not just a local militia. To some degree, it seems to have worked. After the integration, the ING Company has gotten a little more professional. A lot of the new ING guys are Shiites from the south and feel as safe in the city as we do, so they're more prone to do their jobs. Now that things have changed, I expect to see them being targeted more often.

The vehicle was a pickup truck with the back window completely shot out. The driver of the truck must have been returning from a trip to the market, because it was loaded to the brim with cartons of eggs, cigarettes, and other goodies. On closer inspection, it looked like there must have been more than one person in the truck. There was blood and what looked like brains all over the back seat, along with bullet holes all over the side and interior of the truck. We stopped a couple cars on Mobile to question them but didn't get any useful information. After blowing up a couple pieces of UXO that were lying around, we loaded back into the vehicles and left. On the way out, we swung by the nearby gas station to question the attendants, but still didn't get any info.

We started to head east on Mobile, back to the JBCC. On the way, we stopped to take a look at a Land Rover which was pulled over on the side of the road. Apparently the guy at the gas station had mentioned something about it, but we weren't exactly sure what he'd been trying to say. We didn't have a real translator with us, just one of the grunts who had taken a couple of language classes. At any rate, a Land Rover is a pretty unusual vehicle for our area, so we stopped to look. When we peeked in the back window, we saw wires attached from the dome light, taped down the side of the car, leading to the trunk area. Before I had much of a chance to look it over, the XO yelled "Oh, shit—that's a bomb!" so we quickly jumped back into the Humvee and drove a half click down the road. From there, we called EOD to come take a look. The XO ordered us to race to the gas station and snatch up the attendants that we had questioned earlier. We stormed in and scared the shit out of them. We quickly searched the place and I found an AK hidden under the little bed in the trailer. We then detained them in order for the XO to question them. I was actively questioning them with the XO, which was kind of fun. The main guy kept insisting that it wasn't a bomb and we eventually determined, through hand gestures and the few words that the grunt translator could understand, that the guy's boss is the owner of the car. For some reason, he had been detained by the other team while they were heading back to KV on Mobile, and his car had been left where it was when he was taken. The gas station attendant volunteered to approach the car and prove that it wasn't a bomb, but the XO wouldn't let him. We left to head back to the JBCC before EOD could arrive to confirm whether it was a bomb or not, but after a couple hours we heard a loud boom. Word came over the radio that they had blown it. At the time, we assumed that it must have been a bomb, since EOD blew it up. But on the way back to KV at the end of the rotation, we saw the burnt out shell of the car. The frame was still intact which, considering the payload of the two car bombs I've seen thus far, wouldn't have been the case if it had been filled with explosives. I feel bad for the owner. First he was detained by the Americans, probably because he had a nice car which raised our suspicion. Then when he finally gets released, he'll find that his car has been completely destroyed for being parked on the side of the highway ... right where we forced him to leave it.

We finally got back to the JBCC from that fiasco around 0100. Our plan for election day was to head out from the JBCC at 0400 in order to occupy the Iraqi Police station, located in the center of the city. The idea was that our presence in the city on election day would keep the insurgents' focus off the polling station and on us. I got our claymore mines and demo charges ready in preparation for setting up the defensive perimeter around the IP station, so I didn't get much more than an hour of sleep. Sherman attempted to weld some metal stakes together to make a few hedgehog obstructions (an anti-vehicle obstacle), but the JBCC didn't have the right kind of equipment on hand. We built some makeshift ones with barbed wire holding the stakes in place, but they were more for show. Once we finally got going early the next morning, we were all really tired but excited. I believe we all had the sense that something was likely to happen while we were in the city—it wasn't going to be a typical raid or patrol. We were going to occupy a position smack dab in the middle of the city for the entire day. The Muj would have to attack us, if only to save face with the local populace. They couldn't allow us to set up shop in the middle of their city with impunity.

We left the JBCC and rode to the edge of the city in seven-ton trucks. From there, we quietly patrolled deeper into the city, going through the wadis and alleyways in order to get to the IP station without much noise. Once there, I directed my team and some of the grunts in setting up the claymores, our make-shift hedgehogs, stringing some barbed wire, and laying a couple tire spike strips in front of the entryway to the IP station. After we had finished, the entry was as well protected as was possible. The IP station itself is located on one of the busiest intersections in the city—on Routes Michigan, running east-west, and Market, running south. It's an old fort from the British colonial period, and almost looks like a little castle. It has turrets on each corner and a walkway along the top wall.

Most of the grunts were stationed in the two turrets and walkway that overlook the intersection. As the sun came up things were quiet,

The front of the Ar Rutbah Iraqi Police station that we occupied during the Iraqi national elections of January, 2005.

150

but tense. People started to emerge from their homes and the streets slowly got busier. After seeing our machine guns positioned in the turrets and a line of Marines strung along the upper wall, most people quickly returned indoors. Almost no traffic drove down, what is normally, one of the busiest streets in the city. It was kind of suspenseful, just waiting for something to happen. I expected an RPG, or possibly a VBIED. At the very least I expected the Muj to mortar us. Whenever we stay in one part of the city too long, the insurgents make a point of letting the people know that they're going to put up a fight—if only by taking a symbolic shot at us. By taking such a prominent position in the heart of the city on the day of the national elections, it was a direct challenge. But after the casualties from our boys in Haditha, Parrott, Sherman, and I were hoping they would attack.

As the morning progressed, a group of kids gathered at the front of the IP station and began throwing rocks and chanting. At the time, we were in a small room with the infantry Captain and his radioman—listening to the radio reports from the guys up on the wall. Just as the

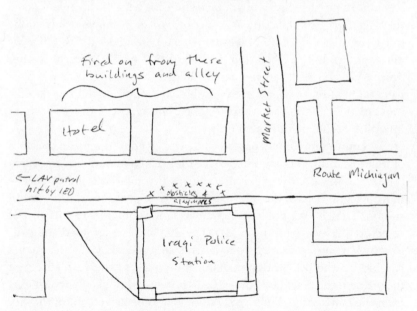

A sketch from the journal of the Iraqi Police station, occupied during the Iraqi national elections of January, 2005.

crowd of kids cleared off, we heard the crackle of small-arms fire. The guys on the wall were taking fire from the alleyways and buildings across the street, on Route Michigan. I was still in the radio room, throwing on my assault pack, when I heard the call "engineers up." The infantry squad on the wall returned fire as we ran to join one of the other squads, preparing to rush out of the IP station. I was pumped as we rushed across the street, ready to blow in some doors and clear the target building on the corner of Michigan and Market. Once we got into position to enter the building, a call came over the radio ordering us not to blow anything if we could possibly avoid it. I'm not sure of the reasoning, but we complied and cleared the building without using any demo. By the time we got into the building and started clearing rooms, anyone that had been shooting at us could have easily run out the back, so we didn't find much. We searched everyone that was in the building but didn't bother detaining any. After that, the infantry Captain told me to extend the defenses around the IP station entrance-way and block the road. We didn't have any more gear with us, so we went into a nearby shop and grabbed some big bags of rice. We stacked the bags in the road, acting as a sort of barrier. It may not have done much, but it would have at least slowed a potential VBIED. Once we got back inside the IP station, we heard that an LAR patrol further down Market Street had been ambushed at the same time as when we were taking fire, so it had been another well-coordinated attack. Like most of their ambushes, they attacked one target with the primary intention of hitting our relief unit.

A couple more hours passed while we stayed stationed on the walls of the IP station, keeping watch over the area. While we had occupied the IP station, LAR was running patrols throughout the city. As the morning progressed, one of the patrols drove past the front of the IP station. They hadn't gone more than a hundred meters to the west of us before they were hit by an IED. The IED blast was immediately fol-lowed by a couple sporadic small-arms shots. Luckily the insurgents had hidden the IED in the median of the road, so the curb absorbed the brunt of the blast. Two of the LAR guys were knocked unconscious from the concussion, but were OK enough to be driven out of the city before being evacuated to KV. A couple more hours passed before we heard a series of thuds. I was back in the radio room at the time and

Marines standing guard in one of the turrets of the Iraqi Police station, occupied during the January, 2005, Iraqi national elections.

my first thought was that it was the grunts on the wall throwing non-lethal grenades. There had been a protest crowd steadily growing in size in front of the IP station and the Captain had explicitly ordered that the crowd not to be allowed to approach the claymore mines, so I assumed they were being warned off. My second thought was that it was the sniper team taking a shot at someone. They had set up a position in the mayor's burnt out office, near the spot where the LAR patrol had been hit by the IED. All of these thoughts occurred in a matter of seconds, as the source of the thuds quickly became obvious. The impacts started to hit and someone yelled "incoming." I've heard mortars being fired fairly often but have never been so close to the Muj's firing position. Parrott and I jumped alongside the wall, waiting for the rest of the impacts. After they all hit, well to our north, we ran up to the front wall facing Michigan.

After getting into position along the wall, the Muj fired another round of mortars, this time landing a little closer. I've come to hate indirect fire, even though the Muj aren't very accurate. Still, I'd almost rather have someone shooting at me; at least then I'd feel like I could fight back. With mortars, all you can do is listen to the booms of the outgoing shots, then sit and wait for the impacts. Following the second round of mortars, the Muj opened up with a smattering of small-arms fire from the buildings directly across Michigan. The M240G on my left returned fire so I started firing too, aiming for the windows of the building directly to my front. In this case, I did what we're trained *not* to do and fired before identifying any good targets. I figured the windows and alley were my best bet. Besides, the Muj haven't been sticking around long after popping off a couple shots, so our best chance would be to return fire immediately. One by one, the power lines running across the street were sawed down from all the fire. After about ten or fifteen seconds, the Captain called a cease-fire.

An infantry squad that had already left the IP station to track down the mortar men, was quickly redirected to assault the building to our front, which was a hotel. They called for engineers, so I yelled for Par-

A view of one of the manned turrets of the Iraqi Police station, occupied during the Iraqi national elections of January, 2005.

rott to follow me across the street. The squad of grunts moving to assault the hotel was coming from behind it, whereas Parrott and I were coming from the front. So we were the only ones running out of the front of the IP station, directly towards the building that had fired on us. On top of that, we were only a hundred yards from where LAR had been hit by an IED only a couple hours earlier. I didn't think about it at the time, but Parrott and I were as exposed as you can get. We ran across the open street as fast as we could. I assume that the insurgents in the hotel had already taken off by the time we ran out of the IP station, just like they had the last time. Otherwise, we were easy targets in the open and they would have fired on us. As we ran, the Captain yelled that they would provide covering fire. I anxiously listened for them to open fire, knowing that if they did, it would mean that they had positively identified targets. Luckily they didn't fire and we were able to join with the squad of grunts on the side of the hotel. Once in position, we rushed in and started methodically clearing rooms.

On the second floor we reached a locked door, so I set a donut charge on the handle and blew it in. It's only a small charge made from just a little bit of det cord, but it blew out all the glass in the windows in that section of the hotel. As we swept into the room, it was strange to see that they had a picture of Muqtada al-Sadr hanging on the wall. That's the second time I've seen his likeness in this area, the other being on a detainees key chain. It's bizarre because he's a Shia cleric and we're in an almost entirely Sunni area. The hotel had a lot of rooms, some of which had military-age men inside, but they all surrendered themselves and offered no resistance. Parrott and I were the first to make it up onto the roof and a hundred yards down Market Street, I saw a guy leaning out of an alley on Market Street, looking towards the IP Station. As quickly as I could, I leaned against the side of the doorway in order to hold my rifle steady from my heavy breathing. As I was raising my rifle, he saw us on the roof and darted back into the alley. It all happened in a split second. I've replayed the event a dozen times in my head and I'm still not sure if I would have actually fired. He wasn't armed and may have just been curiously trying to see what was going on. But after hearing the mortars and shooting, anyone with any common sense should have been locked inside their homes. Instead, this guy was dressed in all black and taking cover, while attempting to see what we were doing. I think I would have been within my rights to have shot him.

At any rate, I felt good and to some degree, seeing some action was cathartic. I felt confident and in control as we were clearing the rooms of the hotel and corralling all the Iraqis that were inside. It took a while to get the entire building cleared, and even longer for the react force to arrive and take away all the Hajjis we had found. We were told that their hands would be tested for gunpowder residue. While we waited, I redirected the claymores and piled more junk in front of the IP station to try and block the road a bit more. The rest of the day was fairly quiet, at least relative to the first half. Towards dusk, one of the M240Gs opened up on some insurgents that were firing on a LAR patrol further down Market Street. Later, the Captain pulled me aside to look into the possibility of blowing a hole in the back wall of the IP station, in case it was needed as an alternate egress route. I told him that I could, but that I wouldn't recommend it. The building is old and the walls would probably collapse. Around 0100 we packed up and patrolled out, heading out of the city and eventually being picked up by the vehicles and brought back to the JBCC.

I was exhausted after we finally got back. Luckily, we didn't have night watch so were able to crash in one of the buildings of the JBCC for the next three hours. I was still tired by the time we were woken up and told to grab our stuff. Apparently, the grunts had been looking for us and were already loaded up to leave. Although I was tired, I still felt wired from the previous day. It felt like we were finally in a standup war—they were attacking, we were counter attacking. At the very least, it took my mind off of the dead and wounded from our platoon. The next day the entire team, with the help of the guys from 1/3, put a cordon around the city—letting no one in or out. The day was much quieter. The JBCC received a few mortar rounds and the Muj took a couple shots at different OPs along the edge of the city, but there were no major attacks. Some of the guys from either 1/3 or LAR were mortared and returned fire after receiving some small-arms fire. In all, it was relatively calm since we didn't get to go back into the center of the city. That night, one of the LAVs at an OP on the north side either had an RPG fired at them, or took some more indirect fire. But we were with the infantry Captain on the south side and spent half of the night racing around the desert, stopping cars that were either trying to leave or come into the city. We heard over the radio that the elections had gone well, and that people were dancing in the streets of Baghdad. Good news, except that in the Ar Rutbah area only one hundred people voted out of an estimated fifty thousand. Of that hundred, most were the ING guys from the south of the country. Apparently the polling station in our AO received a couple rounds of mortar fire, so that may have contributed to keeping voters away.

We spent the majority of the final day of the rotation stopping more vehicles that were attempting to get in or out of the city. At one point, we raced after a car that had sped out of the city and come to a stop at a house on the outskirts. As we were walking up to the house, a dog tried to attack Parrott—snipping at his heals, so he shot it. We called it in over the radio so that the Captain wouldn't worry at the sound of the shot. He called back saying he'd send a medic and a priest. Maybe it was the exhaustion—because it wasn't that funny—but we all laughed our heads off. The Iraqis probably thought we were crazy, we shot their dog and then laughed like maniacs.

We've been told that an ultimatum has been passed to the city leaders: either act peacefully or we will turn Ar Rutbah into the next Fallujah. It'll never happen, but it may just scare them enough to act. Without a doubt, the city leaders know which guys in town are the troublemakers. The remainder of the final day was quiet and we changed over with the other team the next morning. We were all exhausted, but I'm proud of how Parrott, Sherman and I did. After getting back, we heard that we may be sent to Haditha Dam to replace the guys that were wounded and killed. For once, the rumors of a move may be true but we're still waiting to hear.

February 2005:
The Homestretch

Camp Korean Village, Iraq
February 12, 2005

It's been snowing quite a bit, which isn't something that I had expected prior to deployment. There are still rumors circulating that we may be moving to a new area of operations, most likely joining the remainder of our platoon at Haditha Dam. But I would be surprised if we moved so late in the deployment. Besides, if all goes well, we'll be heading back to Al Asad in a couple weeks to start the first leg of the long journey home. We're going out for another rotation tomorrow, so by the time we get back there won't be much combat operations time left before our replacements arrive.

Mom and Dad sent an article that focused on the borders, particularly on the flow of foreign fighters into Iraq. It mentioned that the U.S. has funded the construction of thirty-two forts that are positioned up and down the length of the borders, in order to stem the flow of foreign fighters. It also mentioned that the border crossings at Trebil and Walid have become less and less vital, as evidence suggests that the Muj are simply crossing into Iraq through the open desert. We've flown along this stretch of open desert on helo patrols, and I've seen the long earthen berm that denotes the Iraq side of the desert from that of Syria and Jordan. Apparently, the insurgents have been digging gaps through the berm so that they can simply drive into Iraq, without needing to bother with the border crossing at all. I've also seen one of the forts that the article mentioned, although it didn't look like new construction. I guess that the Iraqis stationed in these forts patrol up and down the berm to search for breaches, but even if they doubled the number of forts, it would be nearly impossible to adequately patrol the endless open desert. I would think that the Muj have a relatively easy time in crossing.

The manner in which the article described our AO, made it sound much more important than it really is. It's funny, if I had read that article at home, I would have thought it was really interesting. But by being here, as a part of the helo and roving patrols that the article described, it's not nearly as exciting as it sounds. In fact, it's not exciting at all. The article made it sound like a tense game of cat and mouse between us and the insurgents. They're trying to sneak in but we're closing in on them—learning their tricks and getting closer each day. If that's really the case, then it must be some other unit. Of course, I haven't spent too much time at either of the borders or at Akashat so it could be true, although I'd be surprised. We've focused almost exclusively on Ar Rutbah and keeping Route Mobile as clear as possible. We have done a couple raids with the Desert Wolves Iraqi unit that the article mentioned, and everyone was impressed. They were much better than any other ING or IP units that I've seen. I was surprised to read that they're Sunnis from Saddam's hometown. We all assumed that they are Shia's from the south. It quoted their commander as saying that they blame Iraq's problems on foreigners, so it makes sense that they would be willing to work to stop the inflow of foreign fighters. Although asking them to join us in fighting Iraqi insurgents may be a different story.

One of the raids we did recently with the Desert Wolves was on the far eastern edge of the city. It was early in the morning, around 0200. Instead of descending on the target houses in vehicles, it was decided that we would approach on foot in order to surprise the people inside, not giving anyone time to slip away. We patrolled around a large hill and then rushed the target houses from the desert. The Desert Wolves led the way and did a good job of quickly putting up a cordon around the target houses. They were as professional as any other unit that we've worked alongside. We pulled some Iraqis out of the buildings and zip tied their hands, assembling them at a collection point in front of one of the houses. The women were crying and the kids looked pretty freaked out. A couple of the Desert Wolves put blankets around the detainees and talked to the women and children to calm them. In that respect, it was particularly nice to do a raid with guys that know the language and understand the culture. Even now, after all the raids we've done, I can't get used to bursting into someone's house and dragging them away.

Camp Korean Village, Iraq
February 27, 2005

The last rotation was pretty interesting. The cordon around the city is still in effect, but has been loosening. We've begun to let traffic in and out and now have VCPs on every road leading into the city. Initially we were searching every car but it created a massive traffic problem, so we now search just enough to keep the Muj guessing. Early in the rotation, we received word that Abu Musab al-Zarqawi was reported to be in our area. We were sitting at one of the VCPs on the east side of the city when a warning came over the radio that a Mercedes would be rolling up to our position. We were told that we should not open fire, as the car contained U.S. troops. Fifteen minutes after the radio warning, a car arrived and a handful of Delta Force guys jumped out. They didn't look like what I had expected. They were just middle-aged guys with beards. I wouldn't think twice if I saw one walking down the street at home—not that that deters from how badass they are.

We spent most of the rotation setting up VCPs with the Delta guys. We conducted one raid which was meant as a diversion. While we did our raid, the Delta guys hit the actual target. We even set up a VCP on Route Mobile, which is something we've never done. There were also a couple drones flying up and down Mobile, which I haven't seen before either. In the end they didn't get him, but it was cool to see those guys in action. On the last night of the rotation, we were told that we should be prepared to go on a raid with them. I'm not sure where the target was, but we were told to be ready "for a long drive." In the end, we didn't go. During the night while I was on watch at an OP on the north side of Mobile, I saw the convoy of Delta guys with their Army Ranger escorts driving away.

A vehicle checkpoint on Route Michigan, on the east side of the city of Ar Rubtah.

One positive that came of the rotation was that some foreign fighters were intercepted after crossing over the border. We had been told that two truckloads of foreign fighters were expected to be crossing into Iraq from Jordan—the intel coming via intercepted cell phone calls. One of the other squads stopped a vehicle and found it packed with fighters. They didn't have weapons yet, because they planned on making their way deeper into Iraq, so were claiming not to be Muj. But it should be easy for HET to pull apart their story. We weren't part of the group that snagged them but, either way, it's a nice way to finish one of our last rotations. We've been told that we may have only one more rotation to go.

* * *

I just found out my Opa (grandfather) died. I received an email from home, telling me to call Dad in Memphis. He died Thursday. When I saw the email asking that I call home, I knew it was something bad. He's been sick for a while and I'd been hoping that he would hold on until I could get home. I wish I had been there.

* * *

I just got back to the tent from calling Memphis. I'd gone into the officers' house to return some gear, when the infantry company XO saw my nametag. He must have recognized it from some kind of family emergency notification, so he passed on the news. Of course I had already heard, but I acted like I hadn't. I was secretly hoping that he would say that I could go home for the funeral but he must have anticipated the question, because after breaking the news he immediately said that there was no way that I could go home. It's what I had assumed and wasn't even going to ask. He gave me a satellite phone to call home, which was nice. I went up to the roof of the building and laid down. After a few tries, I was finally able to get a hold of Dad, and he was able to set up a three-way call with Oma (grandmother). She sounded so sad, the first thing she asked was if I was on my way home. I hated to disappoint her but it was good to talk. After I hung up, I laid on the roof for a while, looking up at the night sky. The only consolation is the knowledge that exactly sixty years ago, Opa was doing the same thing I am now—serving his country, someplace far from home.

The other day, while we were outside the wire, I'd had a very vivid dream in which I saw Opa. I can't remember which night it was, but in the dream I was walking up a stairwell and saw him standing on the stairwell landing. We didn't say anything, but I gave him a hug and he continued climbing up the stairs, and I went down. When I woke up, I had tears on my face—which has never happened before. It still feels strange to think about it now. I don't believe in the supernatural, so I can only chalk it up to a coincidence. Still, in a strange way it feels comforting, like I was able to say goodbye.

Camp Korean Village, Iraq
March 1, 2005

We filled out a health survey last night in preparation for heading home and I was somewhat surprised by our answers. It's easy to see how a doctor or whomever, could read into our answers and think that we have had a harder deployment than the reality. Obviously, I didn't tell the whole truth because I don't want to be held on active duty after we get home. But I can honestly say that I don't think I've changed in any significant way, nor have I seen anything too traumatic. In some ways, the months have just flown by. Every day has been one of two versions of Groundhog Day: either a day inside the wire, or a day outside the wire. At school, there are so many more experiences, both in and outside of class—I'm learning all the time. Whereas here, I feel like I've been through a period of mental stagnation. From the outside looking in it may seem like I've had some interesting experiences, but it doesn't feel that way to me. I would easily trade all the interesting experiences from this year for the standard college experiences that my friends have had.

I answered some parts honestly because I doubt that it will make any difference as to how long we're held on active duty. The questionnaire asked if we've seen dead or wounded enemy, civilians, or Americans. While I've seen some dead bodies, so has almost every Marine in a combat arms unit in Iraq. It didn't bother me at the time, nor does it now. If it had been a dead American then it may have been a different story. In fact, I think I feel more disturbed by seeing the pile of mangled weapons from the helo crash than anything else—just by knowing that each weapon represented a fallen Marine. Still, I consider myself lucky in that the only Marine casualties I've seen have been relatively minor wounded. The questionnaire also asked if we've fired our weapons, or at any time been afraid for our lives. Again, yes to both, but not to a degree that has troubled my mind. It also asked if we held any resentment towards the military, policymakers, or the Iraqis. Through this whole experience, even after losing the guys in our platoon, I don't have any bitterness towards the Iraqis. Frankly, I don't think most of them have any bitterness towards us. They may disagree with our government's policies and wish that we weren't in their country, but I don't think that the majority hate the individual American servicemen or women. The only people I despise, are the ones who want to kill and cause destruction because it's somehow just a part of their DNA. Their declared political objectives are simply a pretext—they'd be making people's lives miserable no matter where they were. But those innately cruel people exist in every society, both Iraqi and American.

I read an article a couple months back that said that 15% of those diagnosed with PTSD hadn't even seen combat. Just the strain of the expectation of combat can cause mental distress. The article then showed a scale, with the percentage of PTSD cases increasing based on the number of combat experiences you've had. The list stopped at five combat experiences, which had an average of 80% of participants reporting some level of PTSD. That seems high, but I suppose that PTSD has a broad scope of symptoms. Some people can no longer function in society, whereas others just feel residual levels of stress and discomfort after getting home. The article didn't really define what constitutes a "combat experience," but I'd say I've had three or four—depending on how they're counted. It also stated that only 20% of U.S. troops deployed to Iraq have seen combat, which again surprised me. I would have thought that it was higher, but I suppose there are a large number of support troops and really quiet AOs.

Camp Korean Village, Iraq
March 5, 2005

We just finished our last rotation. There's the potential that we may be going on one last helo patrol but for all intents and purposes, we're done. It feels weird. In some ways, I never thought it would get here. In others, it seems to have gone so fast. The last rotation was relatively quiet. The city had accepted the ultimatum made after the elections and are willing to cooperate in exchange for a loosening of security. The city also made some demands of their own, which we've accepted. Since that time, things have been much quieter. LAR shot at a guy who was throwing a rock on their last patrol. And one of the grunt squads shot at a car that was accelerating towards their VCP, hitting a little girl who was in the backseat. Because of those two events, we now have to sit through come classes on proper use of force. It seems a bit ridiculous at this point, but I'm past caring.

Before heading back to KV, we rallied up for one last patrol into the city. We drove all the way through town, taking one last tour of the place. When driving through the full length of the city, it struck me as to just how small this place is. We drove down Phoenix, then cut around the intersection and did a short foot patrol. From there, we loaded back into the vehicles and drove over the high bridge, stopping near the ING station. We stood around while the higher-ups went inside, then loaded up again for a vehicle patrol down Michigan. We drove past the IP station, where I was able to snap a photo, before turning around and driving south on Market Street. We exited the city on the southeast side.

It's nice to finally be done. At this point, I feel more tired than happy—a combination of both mental and physical exhaustion. As we were heading back to KV, I sat in the back of a seven-ton and watched the city recede into the distance. I'm sure that I'll never see this place again. This war isn't like Vietnam or World War II, our cultures are too different and we won't be reconciled in thirty years. I don't believe that an American will ever truly be safe in this city, not in my lifetime. Despite what I said in my last entry, I do feel like a different person now. Not in a PTSD sort of way, perhaps just more mature. Some of the experiences have been great. GG, Sherman, Parrott, and I have

A patrol, accompanied by a bomb-sniffing dog, through the city of Ar Rutbah.

grown extremely close over the last few months. Although I'd be surprised if we see each other very often after we get home; nevertheless, I don't think the bond will fade.

Wallace mentioned that most of us will be heading back to Al Asad in helicopters, but that there will also be a convoy. The convoy may go directly to Al Asad, or it may go to Al Asad via Haditha Dam. In any case, one or two of us may go on the convoy. It was probably a stupid thing to do, but I volunteered to go. I guess there's always the chance of getting hit by an IED but for whatever reason, I feel like I've been cooped up in one spot for too long. I wouldn't mind seeing parts of the other AOs. He seemed pretty adamant about going himself, so we'll see how it pans out.

I don't know what to expect when I get home, I don't really feel like partying—I just feel tired. Emily said in an email that her brother sounded sad when he got home, hopefully no one gets that impression of me. I think I'd just like to be by myself for a little while. I know I'll make the rounds visiting friends and family, but I get tired just thinking about it.

Reunited

The March 5 entry was the last I made from Camp Korean Village. Although some portions of the KV garrison returned to Al Asad via convoy, our entire squad boarded transport helicopters for the journey. We were reunited with what remained of our platoon, but for those of us from 2nd squad, it was a bittersweet experience. In the weeks that followed the deaths of Strong, Weaver, Bowling, and Linn, the remainder of our platoon had the time necessary to grow accustomed to the loss. However, those of us in 2nd squad had yet to adjust and were shocked by the emptiness of the reunion. It felt like it wasn't complete and that we were still waiting for the last few guys to join us. For me, everything was overshadowed by this sentiment. I don't believe the platoon was ever fully at ease, at least not in the same manner as prior to the deployment. Although we were happy to be heading home, the fact that we were returning with fewer faces than we had left with made for a gloomy atmosphere. Strong, Weaver, Bowling, and Linn were dead—never to come home. Captain Kuniholm, Meyers, and Miller were back in the States, recovering from severe wounds. When we initially departed from the platoon to head to Camp KV in August 2004, I don't believe anyone would have predicted such a devastating loss.

The final few entries of the journal detail this transition from Al Asad to Kuwait, finally arriving stateside in 29 Palms, California before I made my last entry at home in Virginia. I regret that I didn't better document this period as it was an exciting, emotionally charged experience. Nevertheless, the few entries that I did make are reflective of the strange emotive state that we were all in. While reflective of our losses, we were jubilant to be returning home.

March 2005–April 2005: Heading Home

Al Asad, Iraq
March 13, 2005

We're back in Al Asad now, after having finally linked up with the rest of the platoon. One of the first guys we saw was Frederick. He had been on a vehicle patrol with one of the replacement units, showing them around the AO and as they were riding in a high-back, he leaned over to tell them that they were passing through a particularly dangerous area when an IED went off. No one was killed but a couple were wounded, including him. He has some bandages on his face from some shrapnel. It's the second time he's been wounded, the first was during the ambush in January. This time he likely would have been sent home if we weren't already leaving. I could see bits of grey from the metal still lodged in his temple. Apparently some bits of shrapnel were too jagged and difficult for the docs to risk removing; I know he must be ready to get home.

It felt a little odd when the rest of the platoon finally arrived, at least for the first fifteen minutes. Some of the guys seemed to be jockeying for who had had the more hardcore deployment, telling stories about ambushes or raids. It was such an obvious macho exercise of one-upmanship. I don't really care, nor did most of the guys after the first few stories. We all went where we had been ordered to go, and did what we had been ordered to do. You can't ask for much beyond that. In retrospect, I think I saw a little bit of everything, but not too much of anything. I realize it sounds silly, but I'm glad that I saw some action. Otherwise, I would have spent the rest of my life wondering how I would have responded. Between the rocket attack, IEDs, mortars, car bombs, sniper, RPGs, and a couple ambushes—I believe I now have an answer to that

168

question. I've seen enough to say I've "been there," but not so much that I'm going to have nightmares for the rest of my life. I showed everyone the black Muj hood that I picked up after the ambush in the Triangle. I'm not sure if I'll be allowed to bring it home, since they search our gear before we leave. I plan to roll up the hood and put it in a sock. There's no way to hide the Iraqi Army helmet, so I'll just hope for the best.

The main topic of conversation quickly descended into what exactly happened during the ambush in January. I had a lot of questions about where our guys were killed and how it all went down. Unfortunately, I didn't get too many answers. Most of the guys in the vehicle that night are either dead, or were wounded and sent back to the States. I got the sense that no one wanted to talk about it, so I quickly dropped the subject. I'm guessing they've already been through it ad nauseum and are talked out on the subject. For those of us at KV, we still don't really know how our friends were killed. While nothing can bring them back, for some reason it would be a comfort to know what exactly happened.

In general, talk of the deployment was quickly replaced with what everyone planned to do once they got home. I'm not sure why it surprised me, but we all integrated back together quickly and before long, it was like we had never been separated. I thought that there might have been some kind of divide after having been apart from the platoon for so long. But we all stayed up late that first night, catching up with one another. The little cliques that existed before our squad was separated at the beginning of the deployment were quickly reestablished. I've been hanging around with Miles, Burdette, and Walker. Everyone seems fine, although I think Miles has had a rough time. While Burdette and I were at KV, he and Weaver shared a room together while at Al Asad, so they had gotten really close.

We don't have much to do during the day so we play horseshoes, go to the chow hall, and go to the gym. It's nice to finally be able to relax and hang out with all the guys.

Al Asad, Iraq
March 18, 2005

Since we've finished operations, time has been dragging much more slowly than before. We're anxious to get the hell out of here and should be flying to Kuwait sometime soon. We're expecting to get back to the States by the twenty-second, but I'm starting to think that that may be optimistic. Once we get home, we expect to spend at least a week or two in California. We'll attend classes on post traumatic stress, complete some medical checks, and finish some other logistical/admin stuff, before finally heading home. We hope to get to Virginia by April first or second. Once we do, we'll get four days off before we report back to the Drill Center for processing off active duty. That process is expected to take another day or two, so we should be officially cut loose sometime in the first or second week of April. This timeline sounds almost too good to be true. I'm sure that we'll end up getting stuck somewhere along the way, I just hope that it's stateside.

Some of the guys have been going crazy by spending nearly all of their accumulated money on Al Asad, even though there's not that much to buy. Seven months without seeing a bank statement, while the pay has steadily been deposited, has come as a shock to a few of the guys. Apparently Helch bought a Harley Davidson from a dealership that's set up in trailer near the PX. He said that you can pay for it now and pick it up once you arrive back in the States. I haven't bought much other than a few magazines and a couple books, although I did buy some old Saddam-era dinars from one of the Iraqi workers.

Camp Victory, Kuwait
March 20, 2005

Well, we didn't linger in Al Asad long and we've now officially left Iraq. The flight in the C-130 transport plane from Al Asad was miserable. I guess the plane has to gain altitude quickly so that it doesn't risk taking fire from the ground during takeoff, but with the passenger area not pressurized, it was a painful experience. We all felt a ton of pressure in our ears and I thought that my eardrums were going to burst. Miles has cotton in his ears because they started bleeding.

Before we left, I went to see Parrott one last time. He has volunteered to stay for another tour—fucking crazy. I can understand that he wants to be around to help the guys from his original unit who will be taking over our AO. But it now looks like he may be going to Fallujah instead. I hated to leave him there, we've all gotten close over the last few months. He had tried to convince me to stay for another tour after we first heard about the guys being killed in January. At the time, I actually considered it. I couldn't imagine going back to school, pretending that nothing had happened. But now that some time has elapsed, I don't think I could stay. I'm too ready to just get home and take a break. And if I were to stay, I would need to go someplace new. Seven more months in that shithole-of-a-city would be too much, and I'd be too bored. I think Parrott had the same idea, which is why he's going to Fallujah. Apparently, it was really difficult for him to get permission to even stay. You'd think that they would jump at the offer, people aren't exactly lining up to volunteer for a deployment. But none of the officers wants to be the one responsible for allowing someone to stay for back-to-back tours, just in case there's a PTSD issue down the road.

It's nice to be back at Camp Victory in Kuwait. It feels like it's been forever since we were last here. It's also nice to get some good chow. I thought Al Asad was good, but this place is even better. It feels a little strange to not be carrying a rifle everywhere we go, I feel like I'm always forgetting something. It's also *really* nice to see some women again, some of the guys are chomping at the bit. I'm not quite there yet. I think it'll take me a couple more weeks before I get to the point where things like that become important again. I'm still struggling with that empty, hollow feeling. With so many guys not with us anymore, it's just hard to think that anything else could matter. While I'm happy to be going home, I think I'm sad more than anything.

Camp Victory, Kuwait
March 21, 2005

We're still killing time in Kuwait but should be leaving tonight. My roommates at JMU are throwing a big party on April second. They said that it's in my honor, but I have the sneaking suspicion that this was planned well before they knew that I would be home. Besides, I'm not sure that we'll even be back in Virginia by that time. Even if we are, I probably won't go. I don't think anyone would let me stand around without a drink in my hand, and I don't want to get drunk and ramble about Iraq. For some reason, I feel like it would only cheapen the memories of the guys that were killed. Besides, leaving my family on one of my first nights back home would be a shitty thing to do.

29 Palms, CA
March 29, 2005

We've been in California for a while now. The flight back was really nice, all us NCOs got to sit on the upper level in the business class seats. Miles and I had our pictures taken in the cockpit; a little hokey, but what the hell. We landed at the exact spot where we had taken off from seven months ago. A line of officers shook each of our hands as we got off the plane. Some of the guys in the platoon were acting cavalier about "higher-ups coming to see the guys who have been doing the fighting," but I thought it was a nice gesture. People find a reason to complain about anything. Besides, it's not like we're returning from storming the beaches of Normandy. If we had gotten off the plane and there had been no one to welcome us back to U.S. soil, then I would have been bitter.

After standing around for a while, we loaded onto buses for the drive to 29 Palms. Some of the infantry guys were excited because their families were meeting them there. As far as I know, no one in our platoon had any family waiting for them, so we were a little more subdued. Some of the guys increasingly got on my nerves by making non-stop jokes about shooting at cars that got too close to our bus. Just give it a rest. Still, the bus ride back to 29 Palms was the best part of our return thus far. I hadn't expected anything beyond the greeting that we got immediately after landing, and just assumed that we would be dropped off at our barracks without any fanfare. Instead, the entire population of the town outside the base seemed to turn out for our return. They lined the streets, waving flags and cheering. A guy even rode by on a horse, waving his hat. I can't overstate how good this made all of us feel. I don't know if it was the show of appreciation, the acknowledgment of what we had been through, or just the knowledge that we were once again among our own people—but the simple act of stepping outside to wave to us had more of an emotional impact than I can describe. It was made all the more touching by the fact that we didn't expect it, and by the knowledge that they must to do this for every unit that returns home. Most of all, it was just good to know that people care. What probably seemed like a minor act of kindness on behalf of the people that welcomed us home, is something that I'll remember for the rest of my life.

The next few days were relaxing. We've had a few classes and administrative tasks during the day, but otherwise have had a pretty open schedule. My guess is that this is intentional, as a means to give us time to unwind together. I'm still a little worried that we'll be stuck in some kind of administrative or logistical limbo for days, if not weeks. I just want to get home. We've been told that the Marine Corps has a carefully planned post-deployment "cool down" process, which is meant to allow us the time needed to unwind and assimilate back into life outside of a combat zone. We spend most nights drinking and shooting-the-shit. Some of the guys are hardcore and start drinking again as soon as they wake up. I'm in a room with Burdette and we've had some good nights. The other night, nearly the entire platoon went to the bowling alley in town and stayed until closing time. Burdette wandered off at one point and we couldn't find him when we left. I woke up early in the morning as he was making his way to his rack, covered in dirt and wearing bowling shoes.

A handful have gotten tattoos with the initials of the guys that were killed. There are three designs that have been most popular: (1) the standard Marine Corps Eagle, Globe and Anchor, (2) the engineer castle, and (3) the boots, helmet and rifle motif. Burdette got a barbwire tattoo around his arm, which he is convinced looks crooked. I thought about getting something but can't bring myself to decide. As much as I would like to memorialize the guys in some way, I'm not sure that I want that constant reminder literally tattooed on my body.

The other night, a group of us including Burdette and Miles, were sitting around in our room drinking, when the *Pearl Jam* song "Yellow Ledbetter" came on. It's a sad, slower tempo song which Burdette said was written about the singer's brother, when he was being shipped out for the first Gulf War. It got quiet for a bit, before the conversation made its way to our guys that were killed. We've discussed the events of the ambush before but, until now, no one has mentioned how they feel about it. The song set the mood and it was a charged moment. No one said anything that was ground breaking, but it was cathartic just to talk about them—beyond the details of the ambush. In a way, it was good to know that some of the other guys have been thinking the same things as me. How strange and unfair it feels to be celebrating our return home, knowing that they aren't with us. The knowledge that they were all better people than I, coupled with the sense of relief and guilt at not being one of those killed. I know it's going to take a long time, if ever, for these feelings to fade; but at least I know that I'm not alone.

Williamsburg, VA
April 1, 2005

Home at last. We finally arrived in Lynchburg yesterday evening. We had flown from California, making one brief stop at a decommissioned airfield somewhere in the Midwest before finally landing at the Richmond Airport. On the flight home, SSgt Dreany showed me Miller's helmet, which he is bringing back for him. The Kevlar on the crest of the helmet was frayed and shredded at the points where it had been hit by shrapnel. Once arriving in Richmond, we unloaded onto the tarmac and waited for the buses to arrive. While waiting, I saw Captain Kuniholm for the first time since our squad had been separated. He had a hook in place of his lost arm, but seemed to be doing fine. The other platoons of Charlie Company joined us as we loaded onto buses for the drive to Lynchburg. I was jittery with nervous anticipation the entire drive from Richmond to Lynchburg. As many times as I've driven that stretch of road, I don't think I've ever been so eager to get to my destination. A large part of me doesn't want to go through the process of seeing everyone and catching up, I just want life to go back to normal as quickly as possible.

As we got closer to Lynchburg, a large number of police cars and guys on motorcycles pulled in front and behind of the buses. It must have been a sight, two buses being escorted by over twenty police cars with sirens blaring, and thirty or forty roaring motorcycles. The arrival at the Drill Center was the closest I'll ever come to feeling like a celebrity. There was a massive crowd, and a cheer came up as we pulled into the parking lot. Cameras were flashing and there was even a news crew. All the noise and commotion only made me feel more nervous, though I'm not sure why. For our families, finally seeing those buses arriving had been something that they've dreamed about since we left, whereas I would have been happy to have just been picked up at the airport. After the buses came to a stop, the Staff Sergeants stood at the front to let everyone else off first. Everyone was excited, and it was a stampede to get off the bus as quickly as we could. I had been at the back of the bus and was one of the last to exit. Once I got up to the front, I shook Dreany's hand and hugged Saxo. For some reason, I felt a lingering reluctance. I've always hated attention and just wanted to go from being on the bus, to riding in the car on the way home—without all of the hubbub in between. The reticence subsided as soon as I stepped off the bus and saw Mom and Dad. All the anxiety vanished, and I was just happy to be home.

When I woke up this morning, Mom said she felt bad that I hadn't been able to sleep in. The kitchen is being remodeled and the construction guys were cutting cement blocks early in the morning. I hadn't heard a thing. I slept for almost ten straight hours, probably the best sleep of my life. While I'm happy to be home, there's already a pang of sadness or nostalgia forming with the knowledge that it's all over. We'll head back to the Drill Center to wrap things up but after that, I won't see many of the guys ever again. In some ways, I think that this experience has had more of an impact on my life than many, if not most, other so-called life changing experiences. It's an odd feeling. Finishing high school culminates with a graduation, followed by a transition to the next step in life. But at the end of all of this, there's no big transition. I'll just try to get back to normal.

Postscript

The elections for which my unit helped provide security were intended to build consensus regarding a new Iraqi constitution. While this process was ostensibly intended to be an inclusive one, many Sunni groups feared that if a democratic political process was allowed to proceed, their small numbers would ensure Shiite domination of the government. This general fear was compounded by negotiations between the U.S. military and Shiite groups like Moqtada Sadr's Mahdi army, in which the U.S. essentially paid these groups to lay down their arms. The appearance of collusion between the Americans and the Shiites contributed to the overwhelming majority of Sunnis boycotting the elections, with a national turnout percentage in the single digits, despite Sunnis accounting for roughly twenty percent of the population.

Holding elections was imperative for the overall mission in Iraq for a number of reasons—not the least of which was to signal progress to the American people, who were already growing weary of what was originally supposed to be a brief conflict analogous in scope to Desert Storm. Beyond this, the CPA desperately needed to stand up something approximating an Iraqi-led government, after de–Baathification had gutted many government ministries and disrupted the majority of civil services. There was also likely a desire in the Bush administration to save face after having publicly and repeatedly downplayed the possibility of an Iraqi insurgency.

Unfortunately, instead of fostering reconciliation and national unity, the elections had the opposite effect and caused the widespread disenfranchisement of Iraqi Sunnis from the political process. In short order, there was a spasm of violence in many predominately Sunni areas, particularly in Anbar province. Fighting in places like Ramadi and Fallujah was especially fierce as various Sunni militias targeted Shiite communities and militia groups, as well as against the CPA and U.S. military. This marked a new beginning of the Sunni insurgency that continued largely unabated for several years, and caused some observers to question the viability of the overall American mission in Iraq. During this time, groups like Al Qaeda in Iraq (AQI), led by Abu Musab al-Zarqawi, were able to gain a foothold through a cooperative Sunni populace. However, it wasn't long before many relatively moderate Sunni groups grew weary of the harsh version of Sharia law imposed by AQI, which was characterized by frequent public beheadings, extensive fighting with opposition groups, and a steady stream of foreign fighters.

By 2007, considerable segments of the Sunni population in Anbar had had enough of AQI. They were thus willing to enter the fight against Al Qaeda on the part of the Iraqi government and U.S. military in exchange for remuneration and a place in the political process. This plan was initially opposed by some American policymakers on the grounds that many of these militants had previously fought against the U.S. military. These groups, known as the Sunni Awakening councils, or the Sons of Iraq (SOI), proved to be extremely effective in driving AQI-affiliated groups from Anbar—which was accompanied by a precipitous decline in violence across the province. Though the success of the SOI effectively silenced critics in the United States, it created a separate problem that would have major implications for the growth of the Islamic State years later.

In the early stages of the Sunni Awakening, assurances were made that the Sunnis would have a voice in the Iraqi political process. However, these groups would become victims of their own success; Nouri al Maliki, the Iraqi prime minster at the time, was extremely uncomfortable with the size and capability of the SOI. Rather than integrating them into the Iraqi military, or even sustaining them as an auxiliary security force, Maliki treated them with intense suspicion and sought to marginalize or outright disband them. To be fair to Maliki, these groups had only pledged to fight against AQI—they never pledged allegiance to the Iraqi government—and there is a longstanding history of enmity between Iraq's Shiites and Sunnis. When the U.S. military shifted the financial responsibility of paying the Awakening militias to the Iraqi government, Maliki resisted funding them, and in 2009 the Sunni Awakening began to lose momentum. While Maliki's government agreed to integrate a small percentage of the SOI into the Iraqi military and security forces, the majority remained effectively outside the political fold of the Iraqi state. This left tens of thousands of experienced, well-armed fighters politically disenfranchised, unemployed, and without a role in the country's future.

The problem of how to deal with the Awakening councils was only one of several issues complicating the Sunni-Shia relationship in Iraq, and degrading the security situation in Anbar province. Shortly after the withdrawal of American forces from the country in 2011, Prime Minister Maliki began consolidating Shiite power in earnest, starting with what many viewed as politically-motivated criminal charges against the Sunni Vice President Tariq al-Hashemi. The following year, when Maliki had the bodyguards of the Finance Minister arrested for purported ties to terror groups, there were widespread protests throughout Anbar province, some of which resulted in violence in places like Fallujah and Ramadi.

Concurrent with the deteriorating security situation in Anbar and Kirkuk provinces, the civil war in Syria kicked off in earnest. Elements of AQI that had been seeking refuge from Iraqi security and American forces in the western deserts north of Ar Rutbah moved into eastern Syria under the flag of Al Qaeda—some calling themselves the Al Nusra Front. Many of these fighters were former Baathists with years of combat experience fighting against the American military, Iraqi security forces, and other sectarian militias. Consequently, upon entering Syria these AQI fighters quickly established themselves as the dominant rebel group battling the Syrian military—not simply because of their combat experience, but because of the organizational and military sophistication gained from their time in the Baath party and Saddam Hussein's military. These fighters set their sights on AQI's previous goal of establishing a Sunni caliphate, which had nearly been achieved in western Iraq but was stopped by the 2007 troop surge, along with an aggressive, sustained campaign of direct action raids by Joint Special Operations Command (JSOC) under Gen. McChrystal. Syria's disaffected Sunni population proved to be fertile recruiting ground for IS, as many Sunnis sought revenge for repression at the hand of the ruling Shia Alawites of Bashar al Assad's regime. In addition to the new pool of recruits, financial and material aid for IS began to flow in from throughout the Sunni Arab world. In short order, IS exercised control over huge swaths of Syrian territory—notably in Raqqa, which was the first provincial capital it captured, and where it was first able to establish a de facto state. The success in state-building demonstrated by IS in Syria is a noteworthy divergence from the traditional model of Sunni militant groups, and represented a significant and dangerous evolution, as well as a portent of things to come.

With widespread civil unrest gripping much of Anbar in 2013 and into 2014, Prime Minister Maliki directed security forces to pacify the province, starting with the dismantling of protest camps. Once again, the security forces—which are viewed by many Sunnis as little more than a Shia militia—detained thousands of people on an arguably indiscriminate basis. In some cases, such as in Hawija, confrontations left large numbers of Sunnis dead. This led to an escalating cycle of violence that culminated with IS outright seizing the town of Fallujah and partially seizing the provincial capital, Ramadi. Fighting in the latter would grind on until May 2015. Shortly thereafter, Mosul, Iraq's second largest city fell, followed by much of Diyala, Kirkuk, and Anbar provinces—including Ar Rutbah in June 2014. IS has found considerable support from the Sunni population in some occupied areas, even from those who might otherwise oppose them on ideological grounds, because they view IS as a countervailing force against the Shia-dominated central government.

When the Iraqi army fled from Mosul—despite its significant numerical advantage against the attacking IS forces—it abandoned huge stockpiles of weapons and materiel, including M1A1 Abrams tanks, 155mm artillery, and MRAPs provided by the American military. Despite the escalating crisis in Iraq, the Obama administration was reticent to publicly commit American forces, preferring instead to provide support in the form of shipments of AT-4s, Hellfire missiles, and the like. Such token measures proved to be woefully inadequate to staunch the spread of IS forces. Even the Kurdish Peshmerga forces, which have considerable combat experience and western support, were summarily routed as IS pushed east towards Erbil, the provincial capital of what is commonly known as Iraqi Kurdistan. IS's treatment of captured territory en-route to Erbil was a troubling portent of what would come if the city fell—there were widespread reports of ethnic cleansing and other human rights abuses visited upon ethnic and religious minorities that fell into IS hands. The plight of the Yazidis, many of whom were forced to seek refuge on Sinjar mountain to escape IS, received extensive media coverage in the West. Shortly thereafter, President Obama announced humanitarian aid drops for the Yazidis, accompanied by a campaign of air strikes to beat back IS forces. The latter gradually expanded with the addition of aircraft from Canada, the United Kingdom, and a number of other European countries, and has grown in scope to include targets all over Iraq. To direct these missions, Obama sent small contingents of advisers, but did whatever was possible to avoid committing ground troops in large numbers—the American withdrawal from Iraq being one of the principal achievements of his second term. This has made progress against IS extremely slow as there is no credible ground force to follow the air strikes. The Iraqi army has repeatedly proven itself ineffective in the absence of overwhelming air power. The Peshmerga was able to regroup following its defeat at Mosul, but still lacks the numbers necessary to operate in an offensive capacity.

Behind the scenes, the air campaign came with an important condition: that Nouri al-Maliki relinquish his post. He did, and was replaced by Shiite politician Haider al-Abaddi. Unfortunately, a fresh face in the Prime Minister's office has done little to soothe Shia-Sunni tensions; just as the air campaign has done little to effect a substantial reversal on the battlefield.

Iraq's strategic situation, as well as its long-term viability as a state, is closely linked to internal political events in a number of neighboring states—most notably the four-year Syrian civil war. The regime of Bashar al-Assad exercises no meaningful control, beyond sporadic air attacks, over significant portions of Syria's territory extending from Kobane on the northern border with Turkey, through the province of Raqqa, to Homs on the border with Anbar province. Despite an intensive U.S.-led air campaign throughout Syria, involving forces from several allied countries, little progress has been made in extricating IS. In late September 2015 Russia publicly entered the Syrian conflict by committing both air and ground forces—ostensibly to bolster the Assad regime. This effectively places the United States and its allies in a proxy war with Russia, as Western intelligence agencies and militaries have extensively armed an eclectic mix of Syrian militants from across the ideological spectrum—many of whom are now the target of Russian airstrikes.

The United States, a number of European states including the UK, several Gulf States, and Russia are now involved to varying degrees in what amounts to a complex sectarian transnational civil war. In September 2015 President Obama was forced to reverse what had been one of his principal achievements by publicly recommitting American ground troops to the fight in Iraq. Even so, there is a clear political imperative—one that will almost certainly extend to his successor—to minimize American involvement, at least on the ground, as much as possible. In all likelihood the United States will continue with the politically driven half-measures that so constrained the 2003 Coalition.

Absent a substantial investment of effort, blood, and treasure, it is difficult to foresee a favorable outcome for the people of Iraq.

*   *   *

Warriors leaving a conflict as neither the victor nor the vanquished is a relatively new phenomenon in history. Whether termed as a policing action or as an exercise in nation building, it presents those that return with an interesting, if not slightly bizarre, perspective. Unlike the wars of our forefathers, when we returned home the Iraq War wasn't over; in fact, some of the deadliest fighting would occur in the years following our deployment. Rather, we joined the rest of the American public as mere spectators of a war that, relative to many past wars, had a limited spectatorship. The Iraq War was not a national effort like World War II, nor were its impacts directly felt by the majority of society. For many it was merely a gloomy segment of the daily news roundup. To return to a country that, on the surface, seemed so blissfully ignorant of a war that was being waged in its name was a slightly troubling experience.

I made my last journal entry on April 1, my first day home. We were given four days of leave before returning to the Drill Center in Lynchburg, in order to finish the final paperwork required to process off of active duty. These last few days offered an anti-climactic end to our deployment. We carried on with the humdrum of inventorying gear and making our way through the post-deployment checklist. Some good friends like Miles, Burdette, and GG had finished their terms of enlistment and were leaving the Marine Corps. However, the majority of us still had time—ranging from months to years—on our service contracts. We returned to our schools and jobs with the assumption that we would be deploying again in the near future. As people completed the post deployment out-processing checklist, the Drill Center slowly began to empty until I was one of the last few remaining. It was with a mixture of emotion that I pulled out of the nearly empty parking lot. I knew that this had been an experience that I would remember for the rest of my life. Of all of the fear, excitement, and boredom—the most lasting impact of my deployment was the number of amazing, close friendships that were formed. Some are still close friends, while I haven't spoken with most in many, many years. Nevertheless, the bond formed by this shared experience will remain an important part of my life and I'll always feel a connection to the Marines that I served alongside.

I visited my friends at college shortly after being out-processed. As I pulled into the apartment complex near campus, I sat in my car for several minutes. My heart felt as if it would beat out of my chest and, for a brief moment, I felt like turning around. Starting back at school in the fall offered a similar, anxious experience. I found that I couldn't focus on my schoolwork, which seemed so trivial relative to the war still raging in Iraq. Despite being on a college campus, most of my fellow students didn't know the first thing about the conflict. I, on the other hand, became somewhat obsessed. I checked the casualty reports multiple times a day and read every bit of news and every blog that was available. I was particularly concerned to see casualties in Ar Rutbah begin to increase in the months following our return home. In June 2005—three months after my last combat mission—a LAR Marine was killed by an IED in Ar Rutbah. In the same month, an Army Transport solider was killed by an IED in the vicinity of the city, likely on one of the convoys on Route Mobile. The next month, two more Marines and a soldier were killed near Trebil and later the same month, yet another Marine was killed by an IED in Ar Rutbah. In August, another Army Transport soldier was killed by an IED; followed in October, by two Marines that were killed by small-arms fire in the city. More

Marines and soldiers were killed in the ensuing months, with the reasons ranging from the generic "hostile fire" to IEDs and yet another non-hostile helicopter crash. At the time of our deployment, I questioned the logic behind our aggressive strategy in and around Ar Rutbah. It's a credit to our commanders that aside from the attack on the border, there were no other KIAs or significant WIAs during the deployment—both among the units at KV and the convoys passing through the AO.

Following our return home, I had one year left on my Reserve contract. After we resumed our monthly training, I became increasingly involved in the Reserve unit. I was selected as a trainer for a platoon that was being assembled in anticipation of the next deployment. As by that point, each company in our battalion had served one deployment, it was decided to form a makeshift company by calling for one platoon from each of the individual companies. There was a need for NCO volunteers to deploy with the platoon, since most of the Marines in this makeshift company were those that had not yet deployed. I had recently been promoted to Sergeant and was inclined to volunteer alongside some of the Marines from 2nd Platoon such as Johnson, Sherman, and Parrott—heading out for his third deployment. In the end however, life got in the way and I decided against it.

I finished my enlistment with the Marine Corps before the makeshift platoon returned home. It was an odd feeling, leaving the Drill Center for the final time. I turned in my gear, said good-bye to the dwindling number of familiar faces, and drove away unnoticed in the hustle and bustle of the drill weekend. As I drove home, I tried calling Miles but didn't get an answer, so I drove in silence for the next couple hours. I haven't been back to Lynchburg since, nor have I seen very many of the Marines I served alongside. I still think about my Iraq deployment from time to time, though less often each year.

As I sit at my kitchen table, watching the sun go down over the Rocky Mountains and listening to my kids playing in the next room, I'm struck by a familiar feeling of emptiness and sadness. Both at the futures denied to Brad Arms, Jesse Strong, Chris Weaver, Jonathan Bowling and Karl Linn—as well as for the people of Iraq, most of whom are just trying to survive in a world of seemingly unending violence. I originally set out to document my deployment as a means to memorialize the sacrifices of the Marines of Charlie Company, despite my apprehensions at publishing my private musings. However, through the process I came to the realization that I was being compelled by something more significant. Specifically, the knowledge that my Iraq journal *does not* reflect a unique, or atypical deployment. In fact, it's the opposite. There are literally tens of thousands of men and women who have lived through very similar experiences. Of those many thousands, there are nearly 4,500 who will never return home, or have the chance to tell their own stories. It's to them that I truly want to dedicate this book.

Index